Mountain Tables

Mountain Tables

Tables of the mountain and hill summits of England and Wales

Michael Dewey

Constable London

First published in Great Britain 1995
by Constable and Company Limited
3 The Lanchesters
162 Fulham Palace Road
London W6 9ER
Copyright © 1995 Michael Dewey
ISBN 0 09 474520 X
Set in Times 9pt by
Carreg Limited, Ross-on-Wye, Herefordshire
Printed in Great Britain by
St Edmundsbury Press Ltd, Bury St Edmunds, Suffolk

A CIP catalogue record for this book
is available from the British Library

To Gillian, a companion on all my hill walks

Contents

Introduction and Notes

If you are a keen walker, at some time you will ask yourself, "how many hills have I climbed and how many are there left to climb"? This book will answer such questions and possibly inspire you to explore new hill areas in England and Wales. Included are tables for the two-thousand foot tops, the 500-metre tops, the county tops, Wainwright's Lake District Fells and the notable hills.

The information is presented in three ways -
i.   tables in geographical mountain or hill groups, useful when planning a visit to a particular area;
ii.   tables of mountain or hill tops in order of altitude, to assist the reader with recording summits attained;
iii. tables of tops in alphabetical order, for cross reference purposes.

The majority of heights have been taken from the metric series of 1:25,000 Pathfinder or Outdoor Leisure maps which provide the most up-to-date information. If you are using the 1:50,000 Landranger maps you may discover height differences in my tables. This is due to insufficient space on the Landranger maps to include all height information and some maps still contain spot heights taken from the earlier imperial survey.

If you do attempt the well established challenge of the 2000-footers of England and Wales, there are one or two rules to consider. All walks should start from a metalled road, but this does produce one or two anomalies. Take, for example, Flinty Fell in the Burnhope Seat Group, which has a metalled road running over the fell a few hundred metres from the summit. If you park your car at the top of the road, the intrepid hill-walker has only to go through the gate and walk for five minutes to reach the OS triangulation pillar. I believe you should start ascents from the valley floor and on reaching high ground you can continue to other tops. Using artificial means does not count either, for instance, a car on private or unmetalled roads, a mountain bike or as in the case of

Snowdon and Snaefell, the mountain railway. I leave the reader to determine his or her approach to the task.

I started compiling my England and Wales tables some years ago when it became apparent that, if I wished to climb all the peaks over 2000 feet, I would need to produce an accurate list which drew on the new Ordnance Survey metric maps. While completing the 2000-foot peaks, it was noticeable that good hill-walking country was neglected due to the absence of a 610 metre (2000 foot) contour on OS maps. To overcome this omission I decided to produce a list of 500-metre tops for England and Wales. I believe this is the first published list of this type and, with a 30-metre height difference on all sides, has produced a manageable list of 373 tops.

Many people do not live near the 2000s or 500s and cannot head for the mountains every weekend, therefore I have compiled a list of Notable Hill Tops below 500 metres in altitude. The qualification for a notable hill is purely arbitrary, relying on a hill having a good viewpoint and scope for a pleasant country walk.

A. Wainwright's English Lake District guide books are justifiably very popular and I have listed all of the fells described in his seven Lake District guide books. For those who wish to undertake the challenge, there are 214 fells in total. To climb all the fells described in A.W's books is a delightful task and those who succeed will have wonderful memories of some of the finest mountain scenery in England.

The county tops of England and Wales have also been included. At the time of writing there are plans to return some counties to the much loved pre-1974 boundaries; this table will probably require amending in the future if county boundaries are changed.

Access to the mountains and moorland areas is generally very good. The Lake District, for example, has agreed access for most of the fells above cultivated fields. There are no rights of access to some moorland areas, but landowners usually do not object to the responsible hill-walker who obeys the country code and keeps to paths. It is wise, however, to avoid grouse moors during the shooting season (August to November).

HISTORY OF MOUNTAIN TABLES

The first table of mountain summits in Britain were the Scottish mountains above 3000 feet compiled by Sir Hugh Munro in 1891 and now called The Munros in his honour. With improvements in the Ordnance Survey maps over the years the Munro tables have been regularly revised; currently there are a total of 516 tops in the Scottish Munro tables. Munro's tables now contain other lists of lesser heights, the Corbetts and the Donalds. The Corbetts are Scottish mountains higher than 2500 feet, but below 3000 feet, and the Donalds are the 2000-foot mountains covering the hills of the Southern Uplands.

  The first recorded list of mountain tops in England and Wales was published in 1911 by J Rook-Corbett and contained 130 2500-foot tops. It's interesting to note that the term "peak-bagger" seems to have been in use by this time. The next development was a list of 2000-foot tops of England, published in 1933 by the Rev W. T. Elmslie; his list is based on the then popular Bartholomews half-inch series of maps with the rule for a top being a spot height above 2000 feet. There are one or two entries in the list which are not actual summits: Red Tarn below Helvellyn, for instance, merited an entry. Others were now preparing mountain lists based on the one-inch Ordnance Survey maps, and by the 1940s the Rucksack Club journal had published tables which covered all of England and Wales.

  Until the 1970s no serious attempt had been made to emulate Munro's tables, distinguishing between separate mountains and subsidiary tops. George Bridge in 1973 first undertook the task, developing rules for classifying separate and subsidiary mountain tops. I have broadly retained these rules for the 2000s; the changes result mainly from conversion of contour lines and heights from imperial to metric measure. Bridge's list contains 408 2000-foot tops, of which 248 are separate mountains. One year later Nick Wright published his list of English 2000s, with a grand total of 345 tops. His definition of a top was the presence of one contour ring above 2000 feet on the Ordnance Survey one-inch map, which raised the count somewhat when compared to Bridge's earlier list. Fifteen years were to pass before the next publication on mountain tops appeared on the scene. In the intervening period the Ordnance Survey had resurveyed the entire country and, using the data, had published a new series of metric maps. In 1989 John and Ann Nuttall published *The Mountains of Wales* (Volume 1) and in the following year *The Mountains of England* (Volume 2), which describes ascents of their 432 2000s using the latest information on the new Ordnance Survey metric maps.

Notes on the Mountain and Moorland Areas of the 2000-Foot and 500-Metre Tops

The Lake District – A compact region containing 170 2000-foot tops, but only 45 500-metre tops. The area gives plenty of scope for the hill-walker, with the 2000s, 500s and the Wainwrights to climb. On the down side, some parts of the Lake District have become too popular, causing congestion and path erosion in what is without doubt the most beautiful part of the English countryside. I have sub-divided the area into seven groups as follows:

Scafell Group - Has the most dramatic rock scenery that the Lake District can offer and with a total of 43 tops is the largest group of the 2000s. Scafell Pike, being the highest mountain in England, takes pride of place. The ascent is often made from Seathwaite, which has the distinction of being the wettest village in England. My preference is the longer walk from Langdale up Rossett Pike to Esk Hause, then heading for Scafell Pike, returning via Esk Pike, Bow Fell and the Band. It was on the Scafell crags that English rock climbing made its mark in the late nineteenth century. The bar of the Wasdale Head Hotel is worth visiting, not only to quench your thirst after a hard day in the hills, but also to see the many relics and photographs of the early pioneers of rock climbing.

The Great Gable Group - The Great Gable fells are located to the west of the region; their remoteness from the main Lake District centres has the advantage of providing greater solitude. Wasdale is a good point of access to these fells, where the deep glacial lake of Wastwater provides a dramatic setting to the dale and Great Gable shows its best profile. Pillar

Rock, located on the northern cliffs of Pillar Fell, is the only 2000 requiring rock climbing skills; it is graded as a difficult scramble and is not easy. If you are an average hill-walker without experience of rock climbing, it is advisable to obtain the services of an experienced rock climber who can drag you safely to the top and back down again. The Mardale round is one of the finest horseshoe walks in the Lake District, starting from Wasdale Head going over Pillar, Red Pike and Yewbarrow.

The Buttermere Group - The rocks of this group are of Skiddaw Slate, which erodes more readily, giving a softer and more rounded appearance than the harder Borrowdale volcanic rocks of nearby Scafell and Helvellyn. With narrow ridges and wide open views, the Buttermere Fells on a clear day provide unsurpassed walking. The Newlands round is a favourite walk, taking in Robinson, Hindscarth, Dale Head and High Spy. This route is a fine introduction to the Lakes. The walking is relatively easy and, if the weather is poor, route finding should not be a problem. Keswick and Buttermere are good centres for exploration.

The Skiddaw Group - Skiddaw is sometimes affectionately known as "the old slag heap". This name derives from the grey broken slates on the higher slopes of the fell, but it has a graceful outline which dominates the busy town of Keswick. Blencathra is the finest mountain in the group; the most interesting ascent can be made from Scales going via the short arête of Sharp Edge, which is a lot easier to cross than it looks. Behind Skiddaw, better known as Back o' Skiddaw, are the gentle Calbeck Fells, where long walks can be made away from the crowds of main Lakeland. The Caldbeck Fells have been mined for many years, yielding a variety of minerals such as tungsten, lead, molybdenum, zinc and bismuth.

The Helvellyn Group - Consists of a long massif rising from Ambleside in the south and ending at Threlkeld in the north. It is the eastern side that holds most interest for the hill-walker, where past glacial action has left a fine collection of crags and arêtes. The Striding Edge is the best known arête; in summer people cross in their droves to make the ascent of Helvellyn, which is probably the most climbed mountain in the Lake District.

The High Street Group - Situated in the east of the Lake District, there are some superb walking routes to be found, such as the round from Hawswater over Rough Crag, High Street and returning via Mardale Ill Bell. The walk may be extended by crossing the Nan Bield Pass to Harter Fell, making for the Branstree ridge and eventually returning to the starting point at the head of Mardale. The Kentmere horseshoe will provide another memorable day out, taking in six tops.

The Coniston Group - A small group by Lake District standards, situated in the south of the region with many excellent walks to undertake. The route to Dow Crag via the Walna Scar Road, returning by Goat's Water is well recommended and the ascent of Harter Fell will reward the walker with a fine view of Eskdale, Bow Fell and the Crinkle Crags. Coniston Old Man has been extensively quarried and mined over the centuries, adding a certain character to the fell, and during your walk to the summit you can take time out to explore the workings.

The Cheviots and Northern Pennines - The Cheviots have been included here for geographical convenience, but geologically and physically the Cheviots are separate from the younger Pennine chain. The Northern Pennines form the watershed of northern England; the hills have a wild and desolate air to them, with panoramic vistas and large skies. The valleys are not as attractive as the Yorkshire Dales to the south, but Teesdale is worthy of mention. It is a unique peaceful valley, although in the last century it was an industrial area with many lead mines, but now all is tranquillity and in high summer the fields are covered with rare arctic wild flowers.

The Cheviot Hills Group - The most northerly group, adjoining the Scottish border. The Cheviot Hills consist of granite that formed during the Caledonian orogeny, a large mountain building event that occurred some 400 million years ago. The underlying rock, being impervious to water, has allowed a thick layer of peat to form on the higher ground. Walking over some parts can be heavy going at times, especially along the Pennine Way section leading to the Cheviot. Hedgehope Hill is the best viewpoint, with extensive all-round views, except to the north where the whaleback ridge of the Cheviot obstructs the view. Owing to its location on the Border with Scotland, the area has seen much strife and turmoil in the past. It was infamous for cattle rustling and pillaging, but nowadays it is one of the few National Parks where one can walk a two-thousander with the possibility of not seeing another walker.

The Black Fell Group - To the north of Cross Fell lies the Black Fell Group, an area consisting of grouse moor, where access may be a problem during the months of August to November, the shooting season. Cold Fell is one of the finest tops in the Northern Pennines and on a fine day it is said that you can see the Irish Sea to the west and the North Sea to the east.

The Cross Fell Group - The Cross Fell terrain is predominately moorland, it has the highest ground in the Pennines and there are some excellent long walks available. My last visit was on Little Fell, which is part of the Warcop Training area and is littered with spent artillery shells. There are rights of way over parts of the range and (hopefully) little danger if you obey the red flag warnings, which are located at the main entrances to the range. The Cross Fell ridge is best ascended from the village of Kirkland and in a couple of hours you will be on the highest point of the Pennines. Two miles south of Cross Fell lies Great Dun Fell, easily recognised since a large radar station has unfortunately disfigured the highest section of the Pennines.

The Burnhope Seat Group - Typical Pennine moorland, this group lies to the east of Cross Fell, it is rarely visited and provides the hill-walker with a chance to see wildlife that is sometimes missing from more popular areas. In the summer months I have seen more curlew here than in any other area in Britain. The villages around Burnhope Seat were lively industrial centres a century ago, when lead was mined, but they now have a strange air of desolation.

The Yorkshire Dales and Peak District - Two National Parks cover most of this area of Pennine upland, both quite unique in character. The Yorkshire Dales are well known for the Great Scar limestones, where visitors can explore the limestone pavements and attractions such as Malham Cove and Goredale Scar. The Peak District with its gritstone edges is much frequented by the rock climber because many difficult technical climbs have been developed. The deep limestone valleys of the White Peak to the south are well worth exploring.

The Great Shunner Group - This is Yorkshire Dales country with open vistas and attractive dales. In my opinion Swaledale is the most attractive dale and Wild Boar Fell one of the better tops in the group. To the west of the region are the geologically older Howgill Fells, consisting of Silurian shales, whose graceful outlines can be seen by the north-bound traveller on the M6. It is logical that the Howgills be included in the Shunner Group, even though they have different characteristics to the main Pennine ridge.

The Ingleborough Group - The Ingleborough group is well known for the walk linking the three peaks of Whernside, Ingleborough and Pen-y-gent. The tops are capped with an impervious layer of Millstone grit, where peat is usually abundant; below this layer is the carboniferous limestone. Over the aeons water has percolated through the limestone rocks to form an extensive cave system. The recent ice ages have produced a surface of limestone pavement, where in the summer months rare plant species can be found among the clints and grikes.

The Forest of Bowland Group - Is located to the east of Lancaster, with the reputation of being a "no-go area", and where access to these fells was, until recently, a problem. A number of permitted paths have now been agreed with the local landowners. You can now make the ascent of the three 500s without being accosted by game-keepers. The area is mostly wild moorland used for sheep walk and grouse moor.

The Peak District Group - The Peak District is a large area of upland forming the Southern Pennines to the west of Sheffield and is our most visited National Park with over 10 million visitors per annum. This places great pressure on the fragile upland peat eco-system and to prevent further erosion some paths have had artificial surfaces laid down. In the 1930s, to protect their shooting interests, the landowners prevented access to these hills. It resulted in an organised mass trespass on Kinder Scout with some ramblers ending up in jail. Thanks to that protest, access is now generally very good. The walking here is something to be experienced, with soft peat and deep groughs, with the going difficult especially after a wet period. I have happy memories of the lower half of my body disappearing into a mire of deep peat on Bleaklow on more than one occasion.

Midlands and Southern England - Contains the three remaining high moorland groups in England.

The Long Mynd Group - Consists of several hill areas situated in attractive Welsh Border country. The majority are in Shropshire, but some of the hills stray into Powys. The Long Mynd is a long ridge in the centre, with the Stiperstones and Pontesford Hill forming the upland to the north and west, and the Clee Hills to the southeast. The area is well known for its geology with a complex suite of Pre-Cambrian rocks on the Long Mynd and Ordovician quartzite forming the summit ridge of the Stiperstones.

The Exmoor Group - Is an area of heath and moorland of modest elevation, with only one top exceeding 500 metres. Situated mostly in North Devon, the group is in one of our National Parks. There are many long hill routes and fine coastal walks near by. The area is almost entirely made up of sandstones and shales of Devonian age, being contemporaneous with the Brecon Beacons.

The Dartmoor Group - Dartmoor is Devon's second National Park and is the remains of a high mountain chain formed some 300 million years ago during the Devonian period. The group consists entirely of granite, which is seen at its best on the summit tors. Only one ridge manages to rise above the 2000-foot contour, where High Willhays and Yes Tor are to be found. To make a visit worthwhile and to obtain a better appreciation of this unique granite landscape, the reader could climb some of the 500-metre tops listed in Chapter 2.

North Wales - Boasts the highest hills in England and Wales. Their open and rugged appearance make this true mountaineering country, although the area does not have the scenic prettiness of the Lake District. Over the years Snowdonia has become very popular, with visitors making the pilgrimage either on foot or via the mountain railway to Snowdon, the highest summit in England and Wales.

The Clwydian Hills Group - Located in north-east Wales in the county of Clwyd, it forms a relatively narrow range of hills orientated north to south. These hills are made up of coarse gritstone of Silurian age.

The Hiraethog Group - Located to the east of the Snowdonia National Park, it is not typical of the North Wales landscape, being an area of rolling moorland and forest. The walking can be rough going with large areas of bog and deep heather. It is nevertheless good walking country and certainly worth forsaking the pleasures of Snowdon to walk on lonely Hiraethog.

The Carneddau Group - The Carneddau, located to the north of the Snowdonia National Park, has the largest area above 3000 feet south of the Scottish border. Most of the 3000-foot summits are on a broad stony ridge running north to south. In low cloud it is very easy to become disorientated and lose your way; a compass is essential in case this alarming situation arises. The walks, although long, are not particularly arduous. I recommend a circular walk starting from the eastern end of Llyn Ogwen and following the Afon Lloer north for 1 km, before taking the ridge on the left leading to the summit of Pen yr Ole Wen. The walk then follows the main ridge over Carnedd Dafydd to Carnedd Llywelyn, where you turn right and cross the ridge to Pen yr Helgi Du. The return journey can be made southwards down the broad grassy ridge called Y Braich to the starting point at Llyn Ogwen.

The Glyder Group - Is located to the north of Snowdon, and is known for magnificent glacial cwms, especially on the northern Nant Ffrancon side of the group. The Devil's Kitchen, or Twll Du, is a well-known landmark, where a steep and narrow gully was formed by a cirque glacier. A good walking route passes by the foot of the gully and skirts the left side leading to the col between Y Garn and Glyder Fawr. One of my favourite Welsh mountains is Tryfan and its shark tooth profile is best seen from Pen yr Ole Wen on the Carneddau. Deep inside Elidir Fawr is the largest man-made cavern in Europe, containing the generators for Dinorwic Pumped Storage Power Station. Marchlyn Mawr is the upper reservoir, located on the western side of Elidir, and has been enlarged, which does spoil the view towards Anglesea; however, all transmission lines are laid underground and, due to careful planning, there has been little impact on the landscape.

The Snowdon Group - With Yr Wyddfa being the highest mountain top in this book, the Snowdon group must take a special place. Snowdon is a grand mountain, but at times can resemble an ants nest when thousands of visitors make for the summit. The best route, undoubtedly, is the Snowdon Horseshoe with the airy ridge of Crib-goch leading to Crib y Ddysgl and Yr Wyddfa. Just below the summit of Yr Wyddfa is the terminus of the Snowdon mountain railway, where the hill-walker can take refreshments, but not, as I discovered one day in January, when the café was under six foot of snow.

The Moel Hebog Group - The Moel Hebog mountains, sometimes known as the Eifionydd Hills, are of modest height compared to the giants of Snowdon and the Glyders to the north, but height alone does not make a mountain. The main northern section of the group is the Nantlle ridge: it has six main summits and the ridge is full of interest from beginning to end. To walk the entire ridge takes about eight hours and is without doubt one of the finest ridge walks in Wales, with steep flanks and crags on both sides. It is recommended.

The Moelwyn Group - The town of Blaenau Ffestiniog, the capital of the Welsh slate industry, is the main centre for the Moelwyns. The mountains have been mined and quarried since the start of the industrial revolution. Quarrying still continues to this day, but on a smaller scale. On the higher ground the older workings are now abandoned and have mellowed with time. If you take the route from Tan-y-grisiau to Moel

Druman you will pass by the remains of disused workings and abandoned miners dwellings, which are well worth investigating and provide a good subject for photography.

The Arenig Group - The mountains of the Arenig are spread out with wild moorland between the major summits. The rocks of this area are Ordovician lavas, ejected from ancient volcanoes. During Ordovician times North Wales was part of an island arc volcanic chain on the edge of a long extinct ocean called the Iapetus. My favourite mountain in this group is Dduallt, which, due to its remoteness, is probably the least visited 2000-foot top in Wales.

The Rhinog Group - Although the Rhinogs are not very high, the scenery is one of dramatic rockscapes and wild goats can often be seen perched on seemingly impossible ledges. The area has a reputation for rough going due to the deep heather and hidden boulders, and is somewhat similar to the mountains of south-west Ireland. It is not too difficult and easy scrambles can be made to reach the summits. The southern tops of Y Llethr and Diffwys are the highest, and are somewhat smoother than the northern tops, which makes progress easier.

The Aran Group - The Arans lie to the east of Cadair Idris, and is the southern boundary of Snowdonia. The principle summit is Aran Fawddwy, which is the highest mountain south of Snowdon. On a clear day the views south from the main Aran ridge are extensive and the Brecon Beacons can be seen. The best approach is made from the foot of the Bwlch y Groes road at Pennant. A fine walk through the gorge of Rhiw March leads you towards the crags of the main Aran ridge, and an easy ascent can be made by crossing Foel Hafod-fynydd, where you head right, to climb a steep grassy rake leading to the summit ridge.

The Berwyn Group - Although the Berwyns belong geographically to North Wales, the hills are typically Mid-Wales in character, with smooth ridges and few rock outcrops. Some of the walking is through thick heather, which can make the going hard, especially where paths are not used or don't exist. The main ridge of Cadair Berwyn is best ascended from Tyn-y-fridd, which is located to the south-east of the main ridge, where a fine horseshoe walk can be made by traversing over Foel Wen to Cadair Berwyn and returning via Moel yr Ewig and Godor.

The Cadair Idris Group - The views from the summit of Cadair Idris are reputed to be the best in Wales. It's a splendid mountain with a seven mile northern escarpment, the longest in England and Wales, showing a superb structure of Ordovician volcanic rocks. The best ascent to Penygadair is via the Minffordd path, which starts on the southern side of the mountain not far from the head of Tan-y-llyn, and taking the ridge over Craig Cwm Amarch, where the view of Cwm Cau is best admired.

Mid- and South Wales - With the magnet of rugged Snowdonia to the north, the moorland hills of Mid-Wales are in comparison empty of people; nevertheless it provides the best wilderness walking in Wales. In contrast, the hills of South Wales are very popular, with the summit of Pen y Fan suffering from erosion problems caused by too many boots.

The Pumlumon Group - Most people will recognise the English spelling "Plynlimon", however I have decided to use the correct Welsh spelling "Pumlumon". The landscape with its grassy slopes does not have the rocky grandeur of Snowdonia, but boasts the source of two important rivers: the Severn and the Wye. Lead mines have left their imprint. If you approach Pumlumon Fawr from Eisteddfa Gurig, you will pass by the remains of an old lead mine which, by 1891, had produced 3270 tons of lead. Here you can search the spoil tips for samples of galena, the main lead mineral.

The Rhayader Group - The Rhayader group is a wild moorland plateau with endless possibilities for the walker. The valleys are especially attractive during the autumn months and are best known for the Elan Valley reservoirs, which were built at the turn of the century to provide water for Birmingham Corporation. There are only three 2000s, but with thirty-five 500s in the group, listed in Chapter 2, giving plenty of scope for the committed hill-walker. Drygarn Fawr is the highest top in the group and the summit boasts a fine collection of well-engineered cairns.

The Radnor Forest Group - The smallest of the 2000-foot groups, situated to the north of the Black Mountains. The centrepiece of the group is the central valley called Harley Dingle, which has for many years been a small-arms firing range. After many visits I have never found the range in use, but, if it is, you should still be able to make the round of the three tops in relative safety.

The Preseli Group - A compact group of hills situated in south-west Wales, located a few miles inland from the Pembrokeshire National Park. The rocks of the Preseli are of Ordovician age, which in places have been intruded by Dolerite sills called Bluestone rock. Stone Age man is presumed to have transported the rock from the Preseli to Wiltshire to form part of Stonehenge's inner circle.

The Black Mountain Group - The Black Mountains are located in south-east Wales. This is my home ground and I have probably walked every route possible. It is a very attractive group of moorland hills with five parallel ridges all of similar height, orientated north-west to south-east. The valleys between the ridges have a patchwork of fields which contrast well against the bare hillsides. The western ridge is my favourite, with Pen Allt Mawr and Pen Cerrig-calch providing fine views to the Brecon Beacons.

The Brecon Beacons Group - The Brecon Beacons consist entirely of Old Red Sandstone, formed during the Devonian Period some 360 million years ago; these sandstones were derived from the eroding Caledonian Mountains, which were located in the north. The steep escarpments, running for miles, are unique to this part of Wales and best appreciated by traversing the Carmarthen Fan ridge to the west of the region. A popular route to Pen y Fan, the principle summit of South Wales, is made from the Storey Arms on the A470 road, but the true hill-walker wishing to have a scenic walk will climb from the Brecon side, ascending via Bryn Teg and Cribin.

The Isle of Man Group - I have included Snaefell because, it's in the British Isles and has not been included in other mountain lists. There is only one 2000er on the island, so you could include the 500s. If a lengthy stay is contemplated, there are three long-distance paths: the Millennium Way, across the spine of the island, the Raad ny Follian, the coastal path, and the Bayr ny Skeddan in the south. A trip to the island is recommended.

Notes on Mountain Navigation and Safety

Finding your way to a summit when the cloud is down on high ground is usually easy: it's generally a matter of going uphill until the summit ridge is reached. Most navigational errors occur when leaving a summit to descend or continuing to the next top. It is only too easy to head slightly off course; you will be surprised how errors seem to magnify when in hill fog. To ensure that you depart a summit in the correct direction, take a compass bearing of your departing direction as soon as you reach a summit or a known point. If you intend to return the way you came, it's wise to take occasional back bearings during your ascent. A high proportion of hill-walking accidents occur during descent, when you are probably tired and less alert, leading to navigational errors or, worse, injury.

GEOLOGY OF ENGLAND AND WALES - A BRIEF HISTORY

All land is formed by geological forces. A basic understanding of rock types and how they have influenced the diverse topography of Britain will give the reader an added dimension when hill walking.

Period	Start date	Comments
Pre-Cambrian	4700MY	Age of the Earth
	3790MY	Oldest known rocks (recorded in Greenland).
	2900MY	Oldest rocks in Britain, the Lewisian in NW Scotland. Some rocks may be as old as 3300MY.
Cambrian	600MY	Rocks of the Harlech Dome (Rhinogs) deposited. Slates of Llanberis and Blaenau Ffestiniog deposited. Scotland and England separated by large ocean known as the Iapetus.
Ordovician	500MY	Iapetus ocean closing, subduction zone creates island arc volcanoes in Snowdonia and Lake District. Britain located 25° south of the equator.
Silurian	435MY	Basement rocks of the Pennines deposited. Iapetus ocean nearly closed. Marine shales and limestones deposited in Mid-Wales and Welsh Border.

Period	Start date	Comments
Period	*Start date*	*Comments*
Devonian	395MY	North America and Europe collide. Formation of Caledonian Mountains in Scandinavia, Britain and NE America. Caledonian mountains eroded, sands and gravels deposited in Devon, Brecon Beacons and Black Mountains region. Britain now arid, position 15° south of equator.
Carboniferous	345MY	Early land plants appear. Britain moves to equatorial position. Caledonian mountains further reduced by erosion. Limestone, then millstone grit deposited in Pennines. Swamp fauna in parts of Britain, resulting in formation of coal deposits.
Permian	275MY	Start of Hercynian orogeny, African plate moves to American and European plate. Mountains built in Devon and Cornwall, Pennines faulted and folded. Igneous activity produced sills and dykes in northern England, also mineralisation occurs in Cornwall. Supercontinent of Pangea formed, Britain mainly above sea level and has arid desert climate.
Triassic	255MY	The age of reptiles begins. Britain located 15° north of equator, climate warm and arid. Uplands in Cornwall rapidly eroded, new red sandstones deposited. In the Midlands marl is deposited in shallow lakes. Salt evaporites formed in Cheshire.

Period	*Start date*	*Comments*
Jurassic	155MY	Britain 20° north, climate more humid. Pangea started to split apart. Warm, shallow sea covers much of Britain. Limestones deposited in Cotswolds.
Cretaceous	135MY	European and American plates start to split apart. Britain 35° north, climate cool and arid. Clays and sands deposited in SW Britain. Chalk deposited in southern England. Dinosaurs disappear.
Paleocene	67MY	Britain elevated, becomes a landmass of low relief. Climate warm, possibly sub-tropical.
Eocene	54MY	Mammals appear. Volcanic activity in West Scotland and Northern Ireland, as Atlantic ocean opens. Climate in Britain becomes cooler. Italy, a part of the African plate, is driven into Europe. Alpine orogeny starts.
Oligocene	38MY	Gentle folding in southern Britain caused by alpine orogeny.
Miocene	26MY	Fresh movements of old faults in northern England. Alpine orogeny continues.
Pliocene	7MY	Western Britain above sea level, marine deposits in south-east England. Modern mammals evolve.

Period	Start date	Comments
Pleistocene	2MY	Time of the great ice ages, most of Britain covered by ice sheets up to 8000 feet in depth. Good hill-walking terrain produced!
Holocene	100,000Y	Age of Homo Sapiens.
Present Day		

EXPLANATORY NOTES FOR THE TABLES USED IN THE BOOK

1. *Separate Mountain* - Used only in the 2000-foot tables and listed in descending order of altitude.

2. *Top Number* - Applicable to all mountain tops and listed in descending order of altitude.

3. *Name* - The name of a mountain or hill top as published by the Ordnance Survey (OS). Where a name has not been published on an OS map, I have used a name from an earlier publication. Alternatively, if a name cannot be found, a nearby feature such as a crag or cwm etc has been used. In the 2000-foot list the name shown in brackets indicates a separate mountain belonging to a subsidiary top.

4. *Altitude in Metres* - The heights in my tables are taken from the latest Ordnance Survey maps, the 1/50,000 Landranger series, the 1/25,000 Outdoor Leisure or Pathfinder maps. Where the height of a top cannot be determined by these maps, I consulted the relevant OS 1/10,000 map. Some mountain tops do not have spot heights shown on OS maps; in such cases I have used the highest contour line and added a plus (+) sign to indicate that the height is higher than the contour. It will not be more than the contour height plus nine metres. Some subsidiary tops in the 2000-foot list have been authenticated by Nuttall's own independent survey and for completeness I have included these tops in my tables.

5. *Altitude in Feet* - I have converted the metric heights to imperial using: 1 metre = 3.2808 feet.

6. *Ordnance Survey Map Numbers* - The first column shows the number of the Landranger map whose scale is 1/50,000. The second column shows the Outdoor Leisure map number or, if an Outdoor Leisure map has not been published, a Pathfinder map number. Both of these maps are 1/25,000 scale.

7. *Grid Reference* - I have used the standard OS method of locating a point on a map, by using the six-figure grid reference, being accurate to fifty metres.

8. *Notes* - Information in this column is used for general comments ie. alternative names.

9. The map symbols for the 2000-foot groups are as follows:

KEY TO MAPS SHOWING LOCATION OF MOUNTAIN AND HILL GROUPS

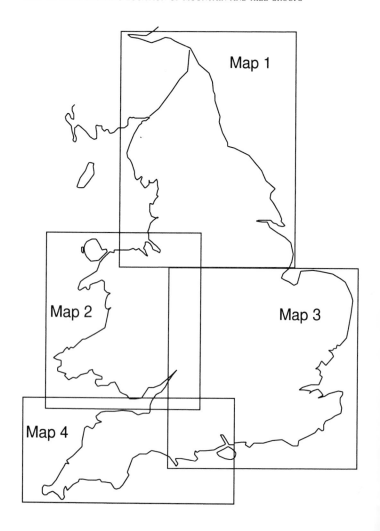

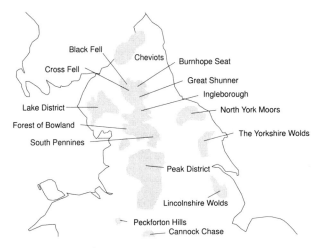

Black Fell
Cheviots
Burnhope Seat
Cross Fell
Great Shunner
Ingleborough
Lake District
North York Moors
Forest of Bowland
The Yorkshire Wolds
South Pennines
Peak District
Lincolnshire Wolds
Peckforton Hills
Cannock Chase

Map 1 Northern England

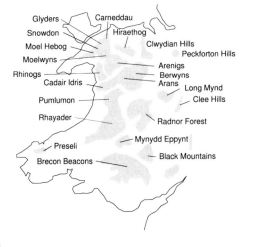

Glyders
Carneddau
Snowdon
Hiraethog
Moel Hebog
Clwydian Hills
Moelwyns
Peckforton Hills
Rhinogs
Arenigs
Cadair Idris
Berwyns
Arans
Long Mynd
Pumlumon
Clee Hills
Rhayader
Radnor Forest
Preseli
Mynydd Eppynt
Brecon Beacons
Black Mountains

Map 2 Wales

Map 3 Southern England

Map 4 South-west England

Chapter 1

The 2000-Foot Mountains of England and Wales

INTRODUCTION

The 2000-foot mountain tops of England and Wales comprise a recognised walking project, although it is not as well known as the Scottish Munros. The advantage of the English and Welsh tops is that they are not as remote or arduous as some of their Scottish counterparts and can be easily reached in a day's walk with no requirement to overnight on the hills. The 2000s are also nearer to the majority of the population in Britain and therefore more accessible. The list is very useful when planning walking holidays, giving you information on the maps required and ideas for exploring new areas.

The thirty-one hill groups in England and Wales have their own tables, and sketch maps providing information about each mountain summit and subsidiary top. I have included a table in order of altitude with space for entering details of personal ascents and a table in alphabetical order for cross reference purposes. Finally I have listed the subsidiary tops included in earlier publications which have been excluded from my list with reasons for deletion.

DEFINITIONS FOR 2000-FOOT MOUNTAIN TOPS

1. *Separate Mountain (top)* - is defined as a mountain exceeding 2000 feet or 610 metres in altitude above mean sea level. It must be separated from *adjacent mountain tops* by a height difference above any intervening col of at least 120 metres at 0.5 kilometres apart; 60 metres at 1 kilometre apart, and pro rata. A *mountain top* beyond 3 kilometres of another top, with at least 15 metres' height difference between its intervening col, will also count as a *separate mountain top*.

Fig 1 below, shows the qualification graph for a separate mountain (top).

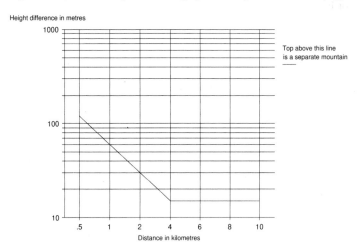

2. *A Subsidiary Mountain (top)* - is defined as a mountain in excess of 2000 feet or 610 metres in altitude that does not qualify as a separate mountain, but has a height difference of at least 15 metres between an intervening col and the adjacent mountain top.

N.B. Example of separate and subsidiary top.

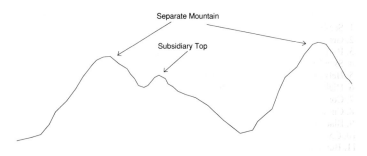

MAP SHOWING LOCATION OF THE 2000-FOOT MOUNTAIN GROUPS
OF ENGLAND AND WALES

1. Scafell	12. Great Shunner	22. Rhinogs
2. Great Gable	13. Ingleborough	23. Arans
3. Buttermere	14. Peak District	24. Berwyns
4. Skiddaw	15. Dartmoor	25. Cadair Idris
5. Helvellyn	16. Carneddau	26. Pumlumon
6. High Street	17. Glyders	27. Rhayader
7. Coniston	18. Snowdon	28. Radnor Forest
8. Cheviots	19. Moel Hebog	29. Black Mountains
9. Black Fell	20. Moelwyns	30. Brecon Beacons
10. Cross Fell	21. Arenigs	31. Isle of Man
11. Burnhope Seat		

TABLES OF THE 2000-FOOT MOUNTAINS IN GROUP ORDER

<u>1. Scafell</u>

Sep Mtn	Top No	Name	Height in Metres	Feet
8	8	Scafell Pike	978	3208
10	10	Sca Fell	964	3162
-	12	Symonds Knott (Scafell Pike)	959	3146
-	16	Ill Crag (Scafell Pike)	935	3067
-	17	Broad Crag (Scafell Pike)	934	3064
19	24	Great End	910	2985
21	26	Bow Fell	902	2959
30	37	Esk Pike	885	2903
-	44	Bowfell - North Top (Bow Fell)	866	2841
37	49	Crinkle Crags	859	2818
-	64	Flesk (Crinkle Crags)	834	2736
-	78	Shelter Crags (Crinkle Crags)	815	2673
64	91	Lingmell	800+	2624+
73	106	Allan Crags	785	2575
75	110	Glaramara	783	2568
-	118	Looking Steads (Glaramara)	775	2542
-	119	Shelter Crag - North Top (Crinkle Crags)	775	2542
88	131	High Raise	762	2500
-	153	Round How (Broad Crag)	741	2431
-	155	Little Stand (Flesk)	740	2427
103	158	Harrison Stickle	736	2414
-	161	Combe Head (Glaramara)	735	2411
-	168	Codale Head (High Raise)	730+	2395+
112	174	Ullscarf	726	2381
-	177	Thunacar Knott (High Raise)	723	2372
-	178	Red Beck Top (Glaramara)	721	2365
-	201	Pike of Stickle (Thunacar Knott)	709	2326
132	207	Pike of Blisco	705	2312
-	212	Middleboot Knotts (Scafell Pike)	703	2306

Grid Ref	Ordnance Map 1/50k	1/25k	
216072	89/90	6	1.
207065	89/90	6	2.
208068	89/90	6	
223074	89/90	6	
219076	89/90	6	
227084	89/90	6	
245064	89/90	6	
237075	89/90	6	
245070	89/90	6	
249049	89/90	6	3.
250046	89/90	6	4.
249053	89/90	6	
209082	89/90	6	
237085	89/90	6	
246105	89/90	4/6	
246102	89/90	4/6	
249057	89/90	6	5.
281095	89/90	4/6	6.
219081	89/90	6	
251034	89/90	6	
282074	89/90	6	
250109	89/90	4/6	
289091	89/90	4/6	
291122	89/90	4	
279080	89/90	6	
243097	89/90	4/6	7.
274074	89/90	6	8.
271042	89/90	6	9.
213081	89/90	6	

Sep Mtn	Top No	Name	Height in Metres	Feet
-	215	Cold Pike (Flesk)	701	2299
-	217	Pavey Ark (Thunacar Knott)	700+	2296+
-	225	Great Knott (Flesk)	696	2283
-	247	High House Tarn Top (Glaramara)	684	2244
-	250	Cold Pike - West Top (Cold Pike)	683	2240
-	254	Loft Crag (Harrison Stickle)	680+	2230+
-	261	Combe Door (Glaramara)	676	2217
-	281	Cold Pike - Far West Top (Cold Pike)	670+	2198+
-	317	Coldbarrow Fell (Ullscarf)	656	2152
-	326	Rossett Pike (Bow Fell)	651	2135
-	352	Dovenest Top (Combe Door)	637	2089
-	368	Seathwaite Fell (Great End)	632	2073
-	369	Seathwaite Fell - South Top (Great End)	631	2070
-	425	Rosthwaite Cam (Dovenest Top)	612	2007

Notes
1. Cumbria County Top
2. Formerly named Scawfell or the Pikes of Scawfell
3. Summit is called Long Top
4. Also named Crinkle Crags South
5. Top named by Nuttall
6. Summit is called High White Stones
7. Top named by Nuttall
8. Also Pike o' Stickle
9. Also named Pike o' Blisco
10. Top named by Nuttall
11. Summit is named Low Saddle
12. Top named by Bridge, Also Cam Crag
13. Also named High House Fell
14. Also named Chapel Fell

Grid Ref	Ordnance Map 1/50k	1/25k	
263036	89/90	6	
285079	89/90	6	
260043	89/90	6	
241092	89/90	4/6	10.
259036	89/90	6	
278071	89/90	6	
253109	89/90	4/6	
256037	89/90	6	
288133	89/90	4	11.
249076	89/90	6	
256114	89/90	4	12.
227097	89/90	4/6	13.
228094	89/90	4/6	
256118	89/90	4	14.

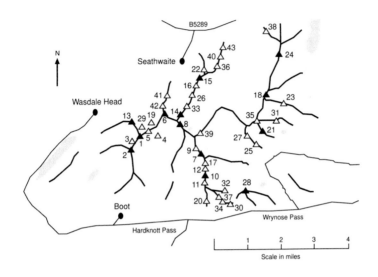

Map of the Scafell Group

1. Scafell Pike
2. Sca Fell
3. Symonds Knott
4. Ill Crag
5. Broad Crag
6. Great End
7. Bow Fell
8. Esk Pike
9. Bowfell - North Top
10. Crinkle Crags
11. Flesk
12. Shelter Crags
13. Lingmell
14. Allan Crags
15. Glaramara

16. Looking Steads
17. Shelter Crags - North Top
18. High Raise
19. Round How
20. Little Stand
21. Harrison Stickle
22. Combe Head
23. Codale Head
24. Ullscarf
25. Thunacar Knott
26. Red Beck Top
27. Pike of Stickle
28. Pike of Blisco
29. Middleboot Knotts
30. Cold Pike

31. Pavey Ark
32. Great Knott
33. High House Tarn Top
34. Cold Pike - West Top
35. Loft Crag
36. Combe Door
37. Cold Pike - Far West Top
38. Coldbarrow Fell
39. Rossett Pike
40. Dovenest Top
41. Seathwaite Fell
42. Seathwaite Fell - South To
43. Rosthwaite Cam

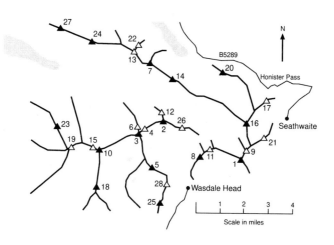

Map of the Great Gable Group

1. Great Gable
2. Pillar
3. Little Scoat Fell
4. Black Crag
5. Red Pike - Wasdale
6. Steeple
7. High Stile
8. Kirk Fell
9. Green Gable
10. Haycock
11. Kirk Fell - East Top
12. Pillar Rock
13. Red Pike - Buttermere
14. High Crag
15. Little Gowder Crag
16. Brandreth
17. Grey Knotts
18. Sea tallen
19. Caw Fell
20. Fleetwith Pike
21. Base Brown
22. Dodd
23. Iron Crag
24. Starling Dodd
25. Yewbarrow
26. Looking Stead
27. Great Borne
28. Stirrup Crag

2. Great Gable

Sep Mtn	Top No	Name	Height in Metres	Feet
22	27	Great Gable	899	2949
26	32	Pillar	892	2926
45	60	Little Scoat Fell	841	2759
-	68	Black Crag (Little Scoat Fell)	828	2716
52	72	Red Pike - Wasdale	826	2709
-	75	Steeple (Little Scoat Fell)	819	2686
57	83	High Stile	807	2647
62	88	Kirk Fell	802	2631
-	90	Green Gable (Great Gable)	801	2627
67	94	Haycock	797	2614
-	105	Kirk Fell - East Top (Kirk Fell)	787	2582
-	113	Pillar Rock (Pillar)	780	2559
-	139	Red Pike - Buttermere (High Stile)	755	2477
100	151	High Crag	744	2440
-	167	Little Gowder Crag (Haycock)	733	2404
119	188	Brandreth	715	2345
-	223	Grey Knotts (Brandreth)	697	2286
145	231	Seatallan	692	2270
-	232	Caw Fell (Haycock)	690+	2263+
208	332	Fleetwith Pike	648	2125
-	335	Base Brown (Green Gable)	646	2119
-	344	Dodd (Red Pike - Buttermere)	641	2103
215	346	Iron Crag	640+	2099+
222	364	Starling Dodd	633	2076
227	378	Yewbarrow	628	2060
-	381	Looking Stead (Pillar)	627	2057
247	411	Great Borne	616	2020
-	413	Stirrup Crag (Yewbarrow)	616	2020

Notes 1. Also named Pillar Fell
      2. Also named Scoat Fell
      3. Name from crag on north side of fell

Grid Ref	Ordnance Map 1/50k	1/25k	
211103	89/90	4/6	
171121	89/90	4	1.
160114	89	4	2.
166116	89	4	3.
165105	89	4/6	
157116	89	4	
170148	89/90	4	
195105	89/90	4/6	
215107	89/90	4/6	
145107	89	4/6	
199107	89/90	4/6	
172124	89/90	4	
161155	89	4	
180140	89/90	4	
140110	89	4/6	
215119	89/90	4	
217126	89/90	4	
139084	89	6	4.
132109	89	4/6	
206142	89/90	4	
225115	89/90	4	
164158	89	4	
123119	89	4	
142157	89	4	
173085	89/90	6	
186118	89/90	4	
124164	89	4	5.
176092	89/90	4/6	6.

4. Formally named Seat Allen - Wainwright
5. Also named Herdus or Herdhouse - Wainwright
6. Also named Yewbarrow North Top - Nuttall

3. Buttermere

Sep Mtn	Top No	Name	Height in Metres	Feet
41	53	Grasmoor	852	2795
47	62	Crag Hill	839	2752
71	103	Grisedale Pike	791	2595
-	120	Sail (Crag Hill)	773	2536
-	121	Wandope (Crag Hill)	772	2532
83	124	Hopegill Head	770	2526
-	137	Sand Hill (Hopegill Head)	756	2480
92	141	Dale Head	753	2470
-	156	Hobcarton Crag (Hopegill Head)	739	2424
102	157	Robinson	737	2417
109	170	Hindscarth	727	2385
-	183	Whiteside - East Top (Hopegill Head)	719	2358
-	205	Whiteside (Whiteside - East Top)	707	2319
-	211	Ladyside Pike (Hopegill Head)	703	2306
173	277	Scar Crags	672	2204
-	308	Whiteless Pike (Wandope)	660	2165
203	323	High Spy	653	2142
-	351	Causey Pike (Scar Crags)	637	2089
-	358	Blea Crag (High Spy)	634	2080
-	360	Hobcarton End (Grisedale Pike)	634	2080

Notes 1. Also named Grassmoor on early maps
2. Also named Eel Crag - Wainwright
3. Also known as Wanlope or Wandhope
4. Also named Hobcarton Pike
5. Also named Lady's Seat - Wainwright
6. Also named Scawdell Fell, Eel Crags or Lobstone Band

Grid Ref	Ordnance Map		
	1/50k	1/25k	
175203	89/90	4	1.
193204	89/90	4	2.
198225	89/90	4	
198203	89/90	4	
188197	89/90	4	3.
186221	89/90	4	4.
187219	89/90	4	
223153	89/90	4	
194220	89/90	4	
202169	89/90	4	
216165	89/90	4	
175221	89/90	4	
171219	89/90	4	
185227	89/90	4	5.
208207	89/90	4	
180189	89/90	4	
234162	89/90	4	6.
219209	89/90	4	
236171	89/90	4	
195235	89/90	4	

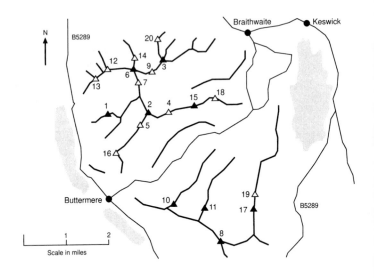

Map of the Buttermere Group

1. Grasmoor
2. Crag Hill
3. Grisdale Pike
4. Sail
5. Wandope
6. Hopegill Head
7. Sand Hill
8. Dale Head
9. Hobcarton Crag
10. Robinson
11. Hindscarth
12. Whiteside - East Top
13. Whiteside
14. Ladyside Pike
15. Scar Crags
16. Whiteless Pike
17. High Spy
18. Causey Pike
19. Blea Crag
20. Hobcarton End

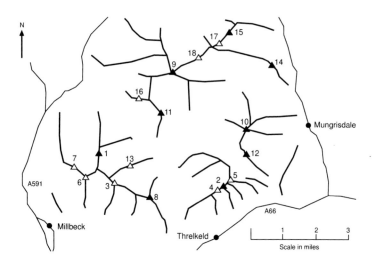

Map of the Skidyaw Group

1. Skiddaw
2. Blencathra
3. Little Man
4. Gategill Fell Top
5. Atkinson Pike
6. Carl Side
7. Long Side
8. Lonscale Fell
9. Knott

10. Bowscale Fell
11. Great Calva
12. Bannerdale Crags
13. Sale How
14. Carrock Fell
15. High Pike
16. Little Calva
17. Hare Stones
18. Great Lingy Hill

4. Skiddaw

Sep Mtn	Top No	Name	Height in Metres	Feet
15	18	Skiddaw	931	3054
34	43	Blencathra	868	2847
35	45	Little Man	865	2837
-	54	Gategill Fell Top (Blencathra)	851	2791
-	57	Atkinson Pike (Blencathra)	845	2772
-	148	Carl Side (Skiddaw)	746	2447
-	165	Long Side (Carl Side)	734	2408
120	189	Lonscale Fell	715	2345
125	197	Knott	710	2329
136	213	Bowscale Fell	702	2303
147	234	Great Calva	690	2263
156	249	Bannerdale Crags	683	2240
-	294	Sale How (Skiddaw)	666	2185
192	305	Carrock Fell	660+	2165+
196	312	High Pike	658	2158
-	343	Little Calva (Great Calva)	642	2106
-	380	Hare Stones (High Pike)	627	2057
-	412	Great Lingy Hill (High Pike)	616	2020

Notes   1. Summit is named Skiddaw Man

2. Also named Saddleback

3. Also named Low Man or Lower Man

4. Top named by Nuttall

5. Summit is named Longside Edge

Grid Ref	Ordnance Map 1/50k	1/25k	
261291	89/90	4	1.
323277	90	4/5	2.
267278	89/90	4	3.
318274	90	4/6	4.
324283	90	4/5	
255281	89/90	4	
249284	89/90	4	5.
285272	89/90	4	
296330	89/90	576	
333306	90	576	
291312	89/90	576	
335290	90	5	
276286	89/90	4	
342336	90	576	
319350	90	576	
282315	89/90	576	
315344	90	576	
310340	90	576	

5. Helvellyn

Sep Mtn	Top No	Name	Height in Metres	Feet
12	13	Helvellyn	950	3116
-	20	Lower Man (Helvellyn)	925	3034
-	33	Nethermost Pike (Helvellyn)	891	2923
27	34	Catstye Cam	890	2919
31	38	Raise	883	2896
32	40	Fairfield	873	2864
-	47	White Side (Raise)	863	2831
-	48	Striding Edge (Helvellyn)	860+	2821+
38	50	Dollywaggon Pike	858	2814
39	51	Great Dodd	857	2811
43	58	Stybarrow Dodd	843	2765
46	61	St Sunday Crag	841	2759
53	73	Hart Crag	822	2696
-	97	Green Side (Stybarrow Dodd)	795	2608
-	100	Dove Crag (Hart Crag)	792	2598
80	117	Red Screes	776	2545
-	128	Great Rigg (Fairfield)	766	2513
-	136	Hart Side (Stybarrow Dodd)	756	2480
104	159	Seat Sandal	736	2414
110	172	Clough Head	726	2381
-	184	Birkhouse Moor (Striding Edge)	718	2355
168	269	Sheffield Pike	675	2214
-	354	Little Hart Crag (Dove Crag)	637	2089
-	389	Birks (St Sunday Crag)	622	2040
-	392	Erne Crag (Great Rigg)	621	2037
-	424	Heron Pike (Great Rigg)	612	2007

Notes   1. Also named Helvellyn Lower Man
2. Also known as Catstycam or Catchedicam - Wainwright
3. Summit is named Whiteside Bank
4. Summit is named High Spying How
5. Also named Great Dod
6. Also named Stybarrow Dod

Grid Ref	Ordnance Map 1/50k	1/25k	
342152	90	5	
337155	90	5	1.
344142	90	5	
348158	90	5	2.
343174	90	5	
359118	90	5	
338167	90	5	3.
351149	90	5	4.
346131	90	5	
342206	90	5	5.
343189	90	5	6.
369134	90	5	7.
368113	90	5	
353188	90	5	8.
375105	90	5/7	
397088	90	7	9.
356104	90	5/7	10.
359197	90	5	
344115	90	5	
334226	90	5	
364159	90	5	
369182	90	5	
387101	90	5/7	
380144	90	5	
357087	90	7	11.
356083	90	7	

7. Summit is named The Cape
8. Summit is named White Stones
9. Also named Kilnshaw Chimney
10. Summit is named Greatrigg Man
11. Name from east side of fell

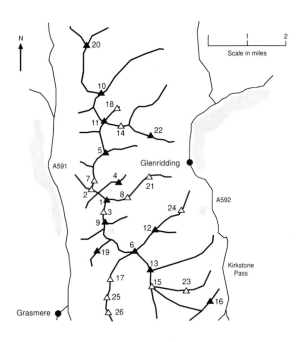

Map of the Helvellyn Group

1. Helvellyn
2. Lower Man
3. Nethermost Pike
4. Catstye Cam
5. Raise
6. Fairfield
7. White Side
8. Striding Edge
9. Dollywaggon Pike
10. Great Dodd
11. Stybarrow Dodd
12. St Sunday Crag
13. Hart Crag
14. Green Side
15. Dove Crag
16. Red Screes
17. Great Rigg
18. Hart Side
19. Seat Sandal
20. Clough Head
21. Birkhouse Moor
22. Sheffield Pike
23. Little Hart Crag
24. Birks
25. Erne Crag
26. Heron Pike

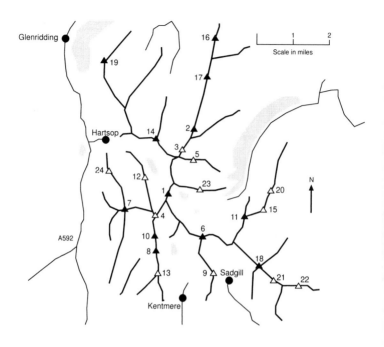

Map of the High Street Group

1. High Street
2. High Raise
3. Rampsgill Head
4. Thornthwaite Crag
5. Kidsty Pike
6. Harter Fell
7. Stony Cove Pike
8. Ill Bell

9. Kentmere Pike
10. Froswick
11. Branstree
12. Gray Crag
13. Yoke
14. Rest Dodd
15. Nowtli Hill
16. Loadpot Hill

17. Wether Hill
18. Tarn Crag
19. Place Fell
20. Selside Pike
21. Grey Crag
22. Harrop Pike
23. Rough Crag
24. Hartsop Dodd

6. High Street

Sep Mtn	Top No	Name	Height in Metres	Feet
51	69	High Street	828	2716
61	87	High Raise	802	2631
-	101	Rampsgill Head (High Raise)	792	2598
-	109	Thornthwaite Crag (High Street)	784	2572
-	112	Kidsty Pike (Rampsgill Head)	780+	2559+
79	116	Harter Fell	778	2552
87	130	Stony Cove Pike	763	2503
90	135	Ill Bell	757	2483
-	169	Kentmere Pike (Harter Fell)	730	2395
115	179	Froswick	720	2362
122	191	Branstree	713	2339
-	196	Gray Crag (Thornthwaite Crag)	710	2329
-	206	Yoke (Ill Bell)	706	2316
142	226	Rest Dodd	696	2283
-	273	Nowtli Hill (Branstree)	673	2208
175	280	Loadpot Hill	671	2201
176	283	Wether Hill	670+	2198+
186	298	Tarn Crag	664	2178
198	316	Place Fell	657	2155
-	320	Selside (Branstree)	655	2148
-	348	Grey Crag (Tarn Crag)	638	2093
-	353	Harrop Pike (Grey Crag)	637	2089
-	377	Rough Crag (High Street)	628	2060
-	406	Hartsop Dodd (Stony Cove Pike)	618	2027

Notes 1. Also named Racecourse Hill
       2. Also named Thornthwaite Beacon
       3. Also named Caudale Moor or John Bell's Banner
       4. Also named Brant Street or Artlecrag Pike
       5. Top named by Bridge, also Artlecrag East

Grid Ref	Ordnance Map 1/50k	1/25k	
441111	90	5	1.
448135	90	5	
443128	90	5	
432101	90	5/7	2.
448126	90	5	
460093	90	5/7	
418100	90	5/7	3.
437077	90	7	
466078	90	7	
435085	90	7	
478100	90	5/7	4.
430110	90	5	
438067	90	7	
433137	90	5	
488104	90	5/7	5.
457181	90	5	
455163	90	5	6.
488078	90	7	
406170	90	5	
490112	90	5	7.
497072	90	7	8.
501078	90	7	
454112	90	5	
411118	90	5	9.

6. Also named Weather Hill
7. Also named Selside Pike
8. Also named Sleddale Fell
9. Also named Round How

7. Coniston

Sep Mtn	Top No	Name	Height in Metres	Feet
59	85	The Old Man of Coniston	803	2634
63	89	Swirl How	802	2631
-	95	Brim Fell (Coniston Old Man)	796	2611
-	107	Great Carrs (Swirl How)	785	2575
78	115	Dow Crag	778	2552
81	122	Grey Friar	770+	2526+
89	132	Wetherlam	762	2500
-	149	Black Sails (Wetherlam)	745	2444
202	322	Harter Fell	653	2142
-	397	Walna Scar (Dow Crag)	621	2037
-	429	White Maiden (Walna Scar)	610+	2001+

Notes   1. Also named Coniston Old Man or The Old Man
        2. Summit is named Little Walls

8. Cheviots

Sep Mtn	Top No	Name	Height in Metres	Feet
55	77	✓ The Cheviot	815	2673
121	190	✓ Hedgehope Hill	714	2342
204	325	✓ Comb Fell	652	2139
243	403	✓ Windy Gyle	619	2030
245	408	Cushat Law	616	2020
256	431	Bloodybush Edge	610	2001

Notes   1. Northumberland county top
        2. Also named Windygate Hill

Grid Ref	Ordnance Map 1/50k	1/25k	
272978	96/97	6	1.
273005	89/90	6	
271986	96/97	6	
271009	89/90	6	
263978	96/97	6	
260004	89/90	6	
288011	89/90	6	2.
283008	89/90	6	
219997	96	6	
258963	96	6	
254957	96	6	

Grid Ref	Ordnance Map 1/50k	1/25k	
909205	74/75	475	1.
944198	80	487	
924187	80	487	
856152	80	487	2.
928138	80	487	
902143	80	487	

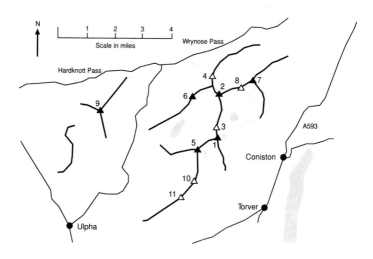

Map of the Coniston Group

1. The Old Man of Coniston
2. Swirl How
3. Brim Fell
4. Great Carrs
5. Dow Crag
6. Grey Friar
7. Wetherlam
8. Black Sails
9. Harter Fell
10. Walna Scar
11. White Maiden

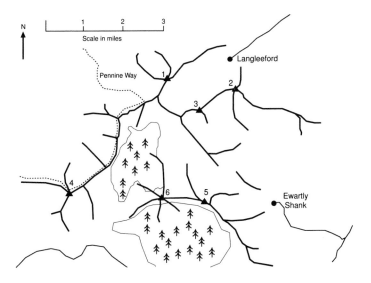

Map of the Cheviot Group

1. The Cheviot
2. Hedgehope Hill
3. Comb Fell
4. Windy Gyle
5. Cushat Law
6. Bloodybush Edge

9. Black Fell

Sep Mtn	Top No	Name	Height in Metres	Feet
185	296	Black Fell	664	2178
199	318	Grey Nag	656	2152
-	355	Tom Smith's Stone Top (Grey Nag)	637	2089
235	391	Cold Fell	621	2037

Notes   1. Summit is named Thornhope Carrs

Map of the Black Fell Group

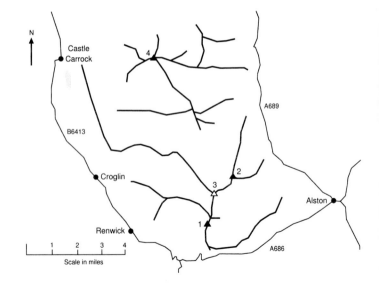

Grid Ref	Ordnance Map 1/50k	1/25k	
648444	86	569	
665476	86	569	1.
655467	86	569	
606556	86	559	

1. Black Fell
2. Grey Nag
3. Tom Smith's Stone Top (Grey Nag)
4. Cold Fell

10. Cross Fell

Sep Mtn	Top No	Name	Height in Metres	Feet
24	29 ✓	Cross Fell	893	2929
42	56 ✓	Great Dun Fell	848	2782
44	59 ✓	Little Dun Fell	842	2762
69	99 ✓	Knock Fell	794	2604
72	104 ✓	Mickle Fell	788	2585
86	127	Meldon Hill	767	2516
99	150	Little Fell	745	2444
128	200	Melmerby Fell	709	2326
139	220	Backstone Edge	699	2293
153	244	Round Hill	686	2250
167	268	Murton Fell	675	2214
-	313	Long Man Hill (Cross Fell)	658	2158
207	331	Viewing Hill	649	2129
219	359	Fiend's Fell	634	2080
239	398	Bellbeaver Rigg	620+	2034+
241	400	Bink Moss	619	2030
-	428	Bullman Hills (Cross Fell)	610+	2001+

Notes   1. Source of the River Tees 1.2km to the east of the summit
2. Also named Green Fell
3. Durham County top, DANGER AREA military range
4. Also named Dufton Fell
5. Also named Burton Fell, DANGER AREA military range

Grid Ref	Ordnance Map 1/50k	1/25k	
687343	91	31	1.
710322	91	31	
704330	91	31	
722303	91	31	2.
804243	91/92	31	3.
771291	91	31	4.
785217	91	31	5.
652380	91	578	6.
726277	91	31	7.
744361	91	31	
754246	91	31	
724373	91	31	
788332	91	31	8.
643406	86	569	9.
763351	91	31	10.
876243	91/92	31	
706374	91	31	

6. Summit is named Dun Edge
7. Name from the scarp the the south of the summit
8. Also named Herdship Fell
9. Also named Gamblesby Allotments
10. Also named Tynehead Fell

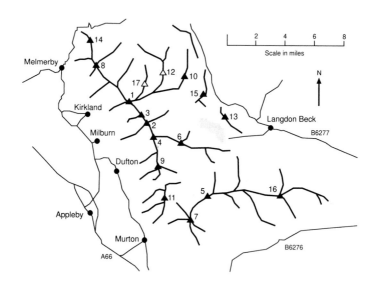

Map of the Cross Fell Group

1. Cross Fell
2. Great Dun Fell
3. Little Dun Fell
4. Knock Fell
5. Mickle Fell
6. Meldon Hill
7. Little Fell
8. Melmerby Fell
9. Backstone Edge
10. Round Hill

11. Murton Fell
12. Long Man Hill
13. Viewing Hill
14. Fiend's Fell
15. Bellbeaver Rigg
16. Bink Moss
17. Bullman Hills

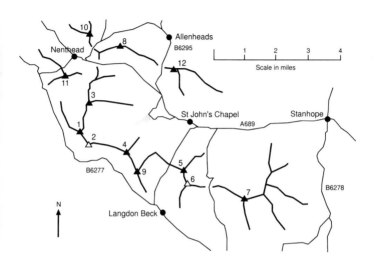

Map of the Burnhope Seat Group

1. Burnhope Seat
2. Redgleam
3. Dead Stones
4. High Field
5. Chapelfell Top
6. Frendrith Hill

7. James's Hill
8. Killhope Law
9. Three Pikes
10. The Dodd
11. Flinty Fell
12. Burtree Fell

11. Burnhope Seat

Sep Mtn	Top No	Name	Height in Metres	Feet
97	146	✓ Burnhope Seat	747	2450
-	186	✓ Redgleam (Burnhope Seat)	718	2355
124	195	Dead Stones	710+	2329+
130	203	✓ High Field	708	2322
135	210	Chapelfell Top	703	2306
-	224	Fendrith Hill (Chapelfell Top)	696	2283
164	265	James's Hill	675	2214
170	272	Killhope Law	673	2208
205	327	Three Pikes	651	2135
248	415	The Dodd	614	2014
250	417	Flinty Fell	614	2014
253	423	Burtree Fell	612	2007

Notes 1. Summit is 300M west of triangulation pillar
2. Also named Harwood Common or Scaud Hill
3. Also named Great Stony Hill
4. Also named Newbiggin Common or Westernhope Moor
5. Also called Middlehope Moor

Grid Ref	Ordnance Map 1/50k	1/25k	
785376	91	31	1.
795363	91	31	2.
794399	91	31	
824359	91/92	31	3.
876346	91/92	31	
877333	91	31	
923326	91/92	31	4.
819448	86/87	31	
834343	91/92	31	
791458	86/87	31	
771420	86/87	31	
862432	87	31	5.

12. Great Shunner

Sep Mtn	Top No	Name	Height in Metres	Feet
118	187 ✓	Great Shunner Fell	716	2349
127	199	High Seat	709	2326
131	204	Wild Boar Fell	708	2322
-	229	Archy Stryrigg (High Seat)	695	2280
-	240	Hugh Seat (High Seat)	689	2260
157	253	Swarth Fell	681	2234
161	259	Tarn Rigg Hill	678	2224
162	260	The Calf	676	2217
-	262	Knoutberry Haw (Tarn Rigg Hill)	676	2217
165	266	Lovely Seat	675	2214
-	270	Calders (The Calf)	674	2211
-	274	Bram Rigg Top (The Calf)	672	2204
172	276	Rogan's Seat	672	2204
-	290	Water Crag (Rogan's Seat)	668	2191
183	293	Sails	667	2188
189	302	Nine Standards Rigg	662	2171
214	345	Fell Head	640+	2099+
216	347	Yarlside	639	2096
232	385	Randygill Top	624	2047
-	386	Bush Howe (The Calf)	623	2043

Notes   1. Summit is named Gregory Chapel
2. Also named Baugh Fell East
3. Also named Hall Moor
4. Summit is named Little Fell Brae

Grid Ref	Ordnance Map 1/50k	1/25k	
849973	98	30	
802012	91/92	608	
758988	98	617	
802003	91/92	608	1.
809991	98	608	
756967	98	617	
741916	98	2	2.
667971	98	617	
731919	98	2	
879950	98	30	
671961	98	617	
668965	98	617	
919031	91/92	30	3.
929046	91/92	30	
809971	98	608	4.
825061	91/92	608	
650982	97	617	
686985	98	617	
687001	91	607	
659981	97	617	

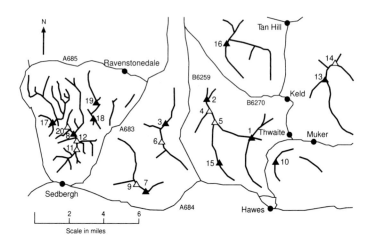

Map of the Great Shunner Group

1. Great Shunner
2. High Seat
3. Wild Boar Fell
4. Archy Styrigg
5. Hugh Seat
6. Swarth Fell
7. Tarn Rigg Hill
8. The Calf
9. Knoutberry How
10. Lovely Seat
11. Calders
12. Bram Rigg Top
13. Rogan's Seat
14. Water Crag
15. Sails
16. Nine Standards Rigg
17. Fell Head
18. Yarlside
19. Randygill Top
20. Bush Howe

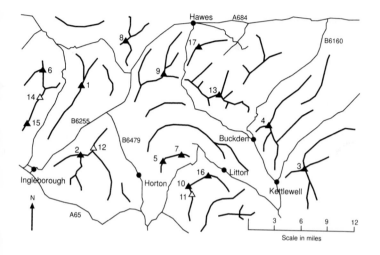

Map of the Ingleborough Group

1. Whernside
2. Ingleborough
3. Great Whernside
4. Buckden Pike
5. Pen-y-gent
6. Great Coum
7. Plover Hill
8. Great Knoutberry Hill
9. Dodd Fell Hill
10. Fountains Fell

11. Fountains Fell - South Top
12. Simon Fell
13. Yockenthwaite Moor
14. Green Hill
15. Gragareth
16. Darnbrook Fell
17. Drumaldrace

13. Ingleborough

Sep Mtn	Top No	Name	Height in Metres	Feet
105	160 ✓	Whernside	736	2414
114	176 ✓	Ingleborough	723	2372
133	208 ✓	Great Whernside	704	2309
137	214 ✓	Buckden Pike	702	2303
144	230 ✓	Pen-y-gent	694	2276
152	243 ✓	Great Coum	687	2254
158	255	Plover Hill	680+	2230+
171	275	Great Knoutberry Hill	672	2204
179	287	Dodd Fell Hill	668	2191
180	289 ✓	Fountains Fell	668	2191
-	301	Fountains Fell - South Top (Fountains Fell)	662	2171
-	330 ✓	Simon Fell (Ingleborough)	650	2132
213	341	Yockenthwaite Moor	643	2109
-	376 ✓	Green Hill (Great Coum)	628	2060
228	379 ✓	Gragareth	627	2057
231	384	Darnbrook Fell	624	2047
249	416	Drumaldrace	614	2014

Notes 1. North Yorkshire county top
2. Also named Ingleborough Hill
3. Also named Buckden Gavel
4. Also named Great Combe

Grid Ref	Ordnance Map 1/50k	1/25k	
738814	98	2	1.
741746	98	2	2.
002739	98	30	
961788	98	30	3.
839734	98	2	
701836	98	2	4.
849752	98	2/30	
789871	98	2	
841846	98	2/30	
865716	98	2	
869708	98	2	
755752	98	30	
909811	98	30	
702820	98	2	5.
688793	98	2	6.
885728	98	30	7.
874867	98	2/30	8.

5. Lancashire county top
6. Also named Greygarth Hill - Bridge
7. Also named Cow Close Fell
8. Also named Wether Fell

14. Peak District

Sep Mtn	Top No	Name	Height in Metres	Feet
217	356 ✓	Kinder Scout	636	2086
221	363 ✓	Bleaklow	633	2076
-	393 ✓	Higher Shelf Stones (Bleaklow)	621	2037

Notes 1. Derbyshire county top
        2. Summit is named Bleaklow Head
        3. Also named Shelf Moor

15. Dartmoor

Sep Mtn	Top No	Name	Height in Metres	Feet
236	394 ✓	High Willhays	621	2037
-	405 ✓	Yes Tor (High Willhays)	619	2030

Notes 1. Devon county top

Grid Ref	Ordnance Map 1/50k	1/25k	
085875	110	1	1.
092959	110	1	2.
089947	110	1	3.

Grid Ref	Ordnance Map 1/50k	1/25k	
580892	191	28	1.
581901	191	28	

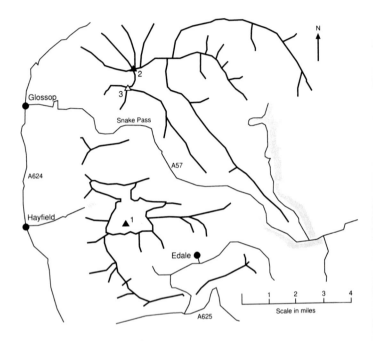

Map of the Peak District Group

1. Kinder Scout
2. Bleaklow
3. Higher Shelf Stones

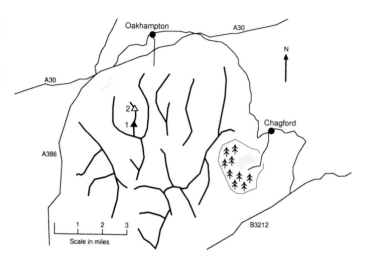

Map of the Dartmoor Group

1. High Willhays
2. Yes Tor

16. Carneddau

Sep Mtn	Top No	Name	Height in Metres	Feet
3	3	Carnedd Llywelyn	1064	3490
4	4	Carnedd Dafydd	1044	3425
7	7	Pen yr Ole Wen	978	3208
9	9	Foel-grach	976	3202
11	11	Yr Elen	962	3156
14	15	Foel-fras	942	3090
-	19	Garnedd Uchaf (Carnedd Llywelyn)	926	3038
-	55	Llwytmor (Foel-fras)	849	2785
48	65	Pen yr Helgi Du	833	2732
-	82	Bera Bach (Garnedd Uchaf)	807	2647
66	93	Pen Llithrig-y-wrach	799	2621
-	98	Bera Mawr (Garnedd Uchaf)	794	2604
82	123	Drum	770	2526
-	134	Drosgl (Garnedd Uchaf)	758	2486
-	162	Craig Eigiau (Foel-grach)	735	2411
-	241	Carnedd y Ddelw (Drum)	688	2257
160	258	Cregiau Gleision	678	2224
-	339	Gyrn Wigau (Drosgl)	643	2109
-	361	Pen Cowlyd (Cregiau Gleision)	634	2080
-	388	Pen y Castell (Drum)	623	2043
258	433	Tal y Fan	610	2001

Notes   1. Also named Pen-yr-oleu-wen

        2. Also named Llwydmor

        3. Also named Penyhelgi-du

Grid Ref	Ordnance Map 1/50k	1/25k	
683645	115	17	
663631	115	17	
656619	115	17	1.
689659	115	17	
673651	115	17	
696682	115	17	
687669	115	17	
689693	115	17	2.
698630	115	17	3.
672678	115	17	
716623	115	17	
675683	115	17	
708696	115	17	4.
664680	115	17	
713654	115	17	5.
708706	115	17	
729615	115	17	
654674	115	17	
734622	115	17	6.
722689	115	17	
729727	115	17	

4. Summit is named Carnedd Penydorth-goch
5. Top named by Nuttall
6. Top named by Bridge after Llyn Cowlyd

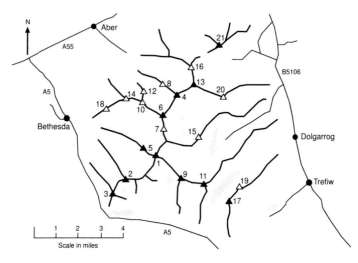

Map of the Carneddau Group

1. Carnedd Llywelyn
2. Carnedd Dafydd
3. Pen yr Ole Wen
4. Foel-grach
5. Yr Elen
6. Foel Fras
7. Garnedd Uchaf
8. Llwytmor
9. Pen yr Helgi-du
10. Bera Bach
11. Pen Llithrig-y-wrach
12. Bera Mawr

13. Drum
14. Drosgl
15. Craig Eigiau
16. Carnedd y Ddelw
17. Craigiau Gleision
18. Gyrn Wigau
19. Pen Cowlyd
20. Pen y Castell
21. Tal y Fan

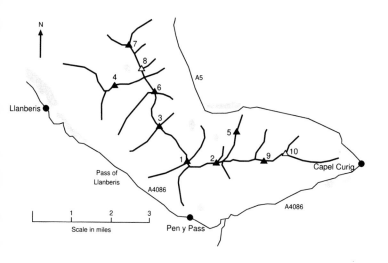

Map of the Glyder Group

1. Glyder Fawr
2. Glyder Fach
3. Y Garn
4. Elidir Fawr
5. Tryfan
6. Foel-goch
7. Carnedd y Filiast
8. Mynydd Perfedd
9. Y Foel-goch
10. Gallt yr Ogof

17. Glyders

Sep Mtn	Top No	Name	Height in Metres	Feet
5	5	Glyder Fawr	999	3277
6	6	Glyder Fach	994	3261
13	14	Y Garn	947	3106
16	21	Elidir Fawr	924	3031
18	23	Tryfan	915	3002
49	66	Foel-goch	831	2726
54	74	Carnedd y Filiast	821	2693
-	79	Mynydd Perfedd (Carnedd y Filiast)	812	2664
58	84	Y Foel-goch	805	2641
-	129	Gallt yr Ogof (Y Foel-goch)	763	2503

Notes 1. Summit is named Y Gwyliwr
2. Formally Trevaen - Thomas Pennant
3. Top named Nant yr Ogof by Bridge

Grid Ref	Ordnance Map		
	1/50k	1/25k	
642579	115	17	
656583	115	17	1.
631596	115	17	
612613	115	17	
664594	115	17	2.
629612	115	17	
621628	115	17	
623619	115	17	
678582	115	17	3.
685586	115	17	

18. Snowdon

Sep Mtn	Top No	Name	Height in Metres	Feet
1	1	Yr Wyddfa	1085	3559
2	2	Crib y Ddysgl	1065	3494
17	22	Crib-goch	923	3028
23	28	Y Lliwedd	898	2946
-	31	Y Lliwedd - East Top (Y Lliwedd)	893	2929
-	76	Lliwedd Bach (Y Lliwedd - East Top)	818	2683
98	147	Yr Aran	747	2450
111	173	Moel Eilio	726	2381
-	185	Llechog (Crib y Ddysgl)	718	2355
169	271	Moel Cynghorion	674	2211
-	374	Foel-gron (Moel Eilio)	629	2063
-	402	Gallt y Wenallt (Lliwedd Bach)	619	2030

Notes 1. Also named Mount Snowdon, Gwynedd county top
       2. Also named Garnedd Ugain
       3. Also named Moel y Cynghorion

Grid Ref	Ordnance Map		
	1/50k	1/25k	
610544	115	17	1.
611552	115	17	2.
624553	115	17	
623534	115	17	
624533	115	17	
628532	115	17	
604515	115	17	
556577	115	17	
606568	115	17	
587564	115	17	3.
560569	115	17	
642533	115	17	

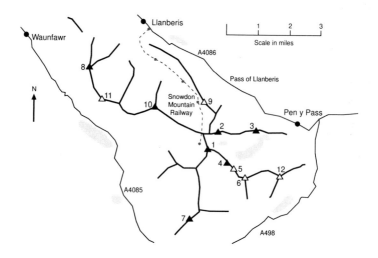

Map of the Snowdon Group

1. Yr Wyddfa
2. Crib y Ddysgl
3. Crib-goch
4. Y Lliwedd
5. Y Lliwedd - East Top
6. Lliwedd Bach

7. Yr Aran
8. Moel Eilio
9. Llechog
10. Moel Cynghorion
11. Foel-gron
12. Gally y Wenallt

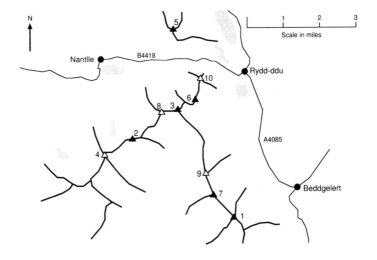

Map of the Moel Hebog Group

1. Moel Hebog
2. Craig Cwm Silyn
3. Trum y Ddysgl
4. Garnedd Goch
5. Mynydd Mawr
6. Mynydd Drws-y-coed
7. Moel yr Ogof
8. Mynydd Tal-y-mignedd
9. Moel Lefn
10. Y Garn

19. Moel Hebog

Sep Mtn	Top No	Name	Height in Metres	Feet
76	111	Moel Hebog	782	2565
106	163	Craig Cwm Silyn	734	2408
129	202	Trum y Ddysgl	709	2326
-	218	Garnedd Goch (Craig Cwm Silyn)	700	2296
141	222	Mynydd Mawr	698	2290
143	228	Mynydd Drws-y-coed	695	2280
200	319	Moel yr Ogof	655	2148
-	324	Mynydd Tal-y-mignedd (Trum y Ddysgl)	653	2142
-	349	Moel Lefn (Moel yr Ogof)	638	2093
-	365	Y Garn (Mynydd Drws-y-coed)	633	2076

Grid Ref	Ordnance Map	
	1/50k	1/25k
565469	115	17
525503	115	17
545516	115	17
511495	115	17
540547	115	17
549518	115	17
556479	115	17
535514	115	17
553486	115	17
551526	115	17

20. Moelwyns

Sep Mtn	Top No	Name	Height in Metres	Feet
33	42	Moel Siabod	872	2860
84	125	Moelwyn Mawr	770	2526
126	198	Moelwyn Bach	710	2329
140	221	Allt-fawr	698	2290
150	237	Cnicht	689	2260
-	238	Craigysgafn (Moelwyn Mawr)	689	2260
163	263	Moel Druman	676	2217
-	278	Ysgafell Wen (Moel Druman)	672	2204
-	286	Ysgafell Wen - North Top (Ysgafell Wen)	669	2194
190	303	Manod Mawr	661	2168
197	314	Manod Mawr - North Top	658	2158
-	328	Ysgafell Wen - Far North Top (Ysgafell)	650+	2132+
210	334	Moel-yr-hydd	648	2125
251	420	Moel Penamnen	614	2014

Notes 1. Summit is named Carnedd Moel-siabod
2. Also named Graig-ddu

Grid Ref	Ordnance Map 1/50k	1/25k	
705546	115	17	1.
658449	124	18	
661438	124	18	
682475	115	17	
645466	115	17	
660443	124	18	
672476	115	17	
667481	115	17	
664486	115	17	
724447	124	18	
728459	115	18	2.
664488	115	17	
672454	115	17	
717483	115	18	

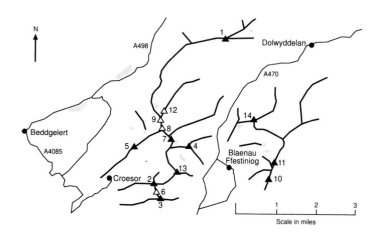

Map of the Moelwyn Group

1. Moel Siabod
2. Moelwyn Mawr
3. Moelwyn Bach
4. Allt-fawr
5. Cnicht
6. Craigysgafn
7. Moel Druman
8. Ysgafell Wen
9. Ysgafell Wen - North Top
10. Manod Mawr

11. Manod Mawr - North Top
12. Ysgafell Wen - Far North Top
13. Moel-yr-hydd
14. Moel Penamnen

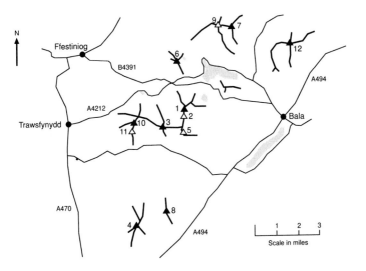

Map of the Arenig Group

1. Arenig Fawr
2. Pen y Diocyn
3. Moel Llyfnant
4. Rhobell Fawr
5. Moel Merddwr
6. Arenig Fach

7. Carnedd y Filiast
8. Dduallt
9. Carnedd Llechwedd-llyfn
10. Gallt y Daren
11. Foel Boeth
12. Foel Goch

21. Arenigs

Sep Mtn	Top No	Name	Height in Metres	Feet
40	52	Arenig Fawr	854	2801
-	63	Pen y Diocyn (Arenig Fawr)	836	2742
94	143	Moel Llyfnant	751	2463
108	166	Rhobell Fawr	734	2408
-	193	Moel Merddwr (Arenig Fawr)	712	2335
149	236	Arenig Fach	689	2260
178	285	Carnedd y Filiast	669	2194
193	306	Dduallt	660+	2165+
-	340	Carnedd Llechwedd-llyfn (Carn' y Filiast)	643	2109
242	401	Gallt y Daren	619	2030
-	409	Foel Boeth (Gallt y Daren)	616	2020
254	427	Foel Goch	611	2004

Notes 1. Summit is named Moel yr Eglwys
2. Top named by Bridge after crag to the south west
3. Authors name from Afon Merddwr the the west
4. Also named Carnedd Bachgen
5. Also named Y Dduallt
6. Also named Gylchedd
7. Principle summit of Foel Boeth

Grid Ref	Ordnance Map 1/50k	1/25k	
827369	124/125	18	1.
827367	124/125	18	2.
809352	124/125	18	
787257	124	23	
827359	124/125	18	3.
820416	124/125	18	4.
871446	124/125	18	
811274	124/125	23	5.
858445	124/125	18	6.
779345	124	18	7.
779342	124	18	
954423	125	18	

22. Rhinogs

Sep Mtn	Top No	Name	Height in Metres	Feet
91	138	Y Llethr	756	2480
95	144	Diffwys	750	2460
116	180	Rhinog Fawr	720	2362
123	194	Rhinog Fach	712	2335
-	282	Crib-y-rhiw (Y Llethr)	670+	2198+
-	342	Craig Bodlyn (Diffwys)	642	2106
226	375	Y Garn	629	2063
233	387	Moel Ysgyfarnogod	623	2043
-	418	Foel Penolau (Moel Ysgyfarnogod)	614	2014

Notes   1. Authors name from crags on north side of ridge

Grid Ref	Ordnance Map		
	1/50k	*1/25k*	
661258	124	18	
661234	124	18	
657290	124	18	
665270	124	18	
664249	124	18	
648229	124	18	1.
703230	124	18	
659346	124	18	
662348	124	18	

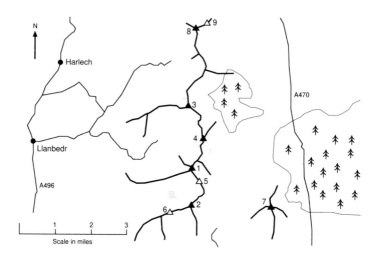

Map of the Rhinog Group

1. Y Llethr
2. Diffwys
3. Rhinog Fawr
4. Rhinog Fach
5. Crib-y-rhiw
6. Craig Bodlyn
7. Y Garn
8. Moel Ysgyfarnogod
9. Foel Penolau

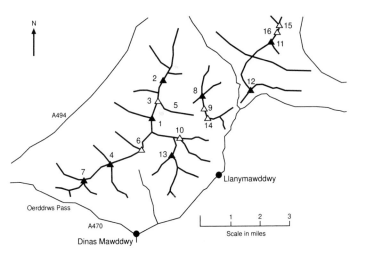

Map of the Aran Group

1. Aran Fawddwy
2. Aran Benllyn
3. Erw y Ddafad-ddu
4. Glasgwm
5. Foel Hafod-fynydd
6. Gwaun y Llwyni
7. Pen y Bryn-fforchog
8. Esgeiriau Gwynion
9. Foel Rhudd
10. Gwaun Lydan

11. Foel y Geifr
12. Moel y Cerrig-duon
13. Pen yr Allt-uchaf
14. Llechwedd Du
15. Foel Goch
16. Trum y Gwrgedd

23. Arans

Sep Mtn	Top No	Name	Height in Metres	Feet
20	25	Aran Fawddwy	905	2969
29	36	Aran Benllyn	885	2903
-	41	Erw y Ddafad-ddu (Aran Fawddwy)	872	2860
77	114	Glasgwm	779	2555
151	239	Foel Hafod-fynydd	689	2260
-	245	Gwaun y Llwyni (Aran Fawddwy)	685	2247
154	246	Pen y Bryn-fforchog	685	2247
174	279	Esgeiriau Gwynion	671	2201
-	310	Foel Rhudd (Esgeiriau Gwynion)	659	2162
-	367	Gwaun Lydan (Aran Fawddwy)	632	2073
229	382	Foel y Geifr	626	2053
230	383	Moel y Cerrig-duon	625	2050
240	399	Pen yr Allt-uchaf	620+	2034+
-	419	Llechwedd Du (Esgeiriau Gwynion)	614	2014
-	421	Foel Goch (Foel y Geifr)	613	2011
-	426	Trum y Gwrgedd (Foel y Geifr)	612	2007

Notes 1. Source of River Dyfi below Aran Fawddwy's eastern crags
2. Also named Craig y Ffynnon
3. Also named Pen Main
4. Also named Pen y Helfa
5. Also named Foel Tycanol
6. Also named Mynydd Carnedd Hywel
7. Also named Graig Ty-nant

Grid Ref	Ordnance Map 1/50k	1/25k	
863224	124/125	23	1.
867243	124/125	23	
865234	124/125	23	
837195	124/125	23	2.
878227	124/125	23	
857205	124/125	23	3.
818179	124/125	23	4.
889236	124/125	23	
896239	124/125	23	
881212	124/125	23	5.
937275	125	23	6.
923241	125	23	
871197	124/125	23	
894224	124/125	23	7.
943291	125	18	
941284	125	23	

24. Berwyns

Sep Mtn	Top No	Name	Height in Metres	Feet
50	67	Cadair Berwyn - South Top	830	2723
-	70	Cadair Berwyn	827	2713
-	71	Moel Sych (Cadair Berwyn - South Top)	827	2713
74	108	Cadair Bronwen	784	2572
-	154	Tomle (Cadair Berwyn)	741	2431
-	219	Pen-y-bryn (Cadair Bronwen)	700	2296
-	227	Moel yr Ewig (Moel Sych)	695	2280
146	233	Foel Wen	690	2263
-	242	Foel Wen - South Top (Foel Wen)	687	2254
-	252	Mynydd Tarw (Foel Wen)	681	2243
-	257	Godor (Moel yr Ewig)	679	2227
-	264	Godor - North Top (Moel yr Ewig)	675	2214
181	291	Cyrniau Nod	667	2188
184	295	Post Gwyn	665	2181
-	311	Y Groes Fagl (Cyrniau Nod)	659	2162
209	333	Foel Cwm Sian-llwyd	648	2125
211	337	Pen y Boncyn Trefeilw	646	2119
-	370	Stack Rhos (Pen y Boncyn Trefeilw)	630+	2066+
224	371	Moel Fferna	630	2066
237	395	Pen Bwlch Llandrillo Top	621	2037
-	414	Cefn Gwyntog (Cyrniau Nod)	615	2017

Notes   1. Clwyd county top
2. Summit is named Bwrdd Arthur
3. Top named by Bridge
4. Named Trum y Sarn by Bridge
5. Top named by Nuttall, also named Y Foel by Bridge

Grid Ref	Ordnance Map 1/50k	1/25k	
072323	125	826	1.
072327	125	826	
066319	125	826	
078347	125	826	2.
085336	125	826	
087352	125	826	3.
081318	125	826	
099334	125	826	
102330	125	826	
113324	125	826	
094307	125	826	
089311	125	826	
989279	125	23	
048294	125	846	
989290	125	825	
996314	125	825	4.
963283	125	23	
969279	125	23	
117398	125	826	
090369	125	826	5.
976266	125	23	

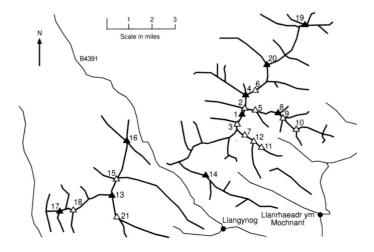

Map of the Berwyn Group

1. Cadair Berwyn - South Top
2. Cadair Berwyn
3. Moel Sych
4. Cadair Bronwen
5. Tomle
6. Pen-y-bryn
7. Moel yr Ewig
8. Foel Wen
9. Foel Wen - South Top
10. Mynydd Tarw
11. Godor
12. Godor - North Top

13. Cyrniau Nod
14. Post Gwyn
15. Y Groes Fagl
16. Foel Cwm Sian-llwyd
17. Pen y Boncyn Trefeilw
18. Stack Rhos
19. Moel Fferna
20. Pen Bwlch Llandrillo Top
21. Cefn Gwyntog

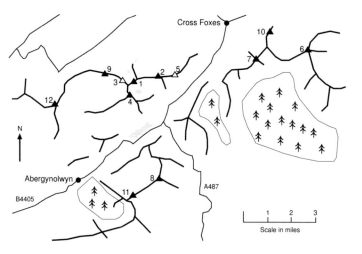

Map of the Cadair Idris Group

1. Cadair Idris
2. Mynydd Moel
3. Cyfwy
4. Craig Cwm Amarch
5. Gau Graig
6. Maesglase

7. Waun-oer
8. Tarren y Gesail
9. Tyrau Mawr
10. Cribin Fawr
11. Tarrenhendre
12. Craig y Llyn

25. Cadair Idris

Sep Mtn	Top No	Name	Height in Metres	Feet
25	30	Cadair Idris	893	2929
36	46	Mynydd Moel	863	2831
-	80	Cyfrwy (Pen y Gadair)	811	2660
70	102	Craig Cwm Amarch	791	2595
-	251	Gau Graig (Mynydd Moel)	683	2240
166	267	Maesglase	675	2214
177	284	Waun-oer	670	2198
182	292	Tarren y Gesail	667	2188
191	304	Tyrau Mawr	661	2168
195	309	Cribin Fawr	659	2162
220	362	Tarrenhendre	634	2080
234	390	Craig y Llyn	622	2040

Notes 1. Summit is named Penygadair
2. Also named The Saddle
3. Also named Mynydd Pencoed
4. Name from the crag on north side of mountain
5. Summit is named Maen Du or Measgasau
6. Summit is named Craig-las

Grid Ref	Ordnance Map 1/50k	1/25k	
711130	124	23	1.
727137	124	23	
704133	124	23	2.
711121	124	23	3.
744141	124	23	4.
823152	124/125	23	5.
786148	124	23	
711059	124	23	
677136	124	23	6.
795153	124	23	
683042	135	23	
666120	124	23	

26. Pumlumon

Sep Mtn	Top No	Name	Height in Metres	Feet
93	142	Pumlumon Fawr	752	2467
101	152	Pen Pumlumon Arwystli	741	2431
-	171	Pen Pumlumon Llygad-bychan (Arwystli)	727	2385
155	248	Y Garn	684	2244
-	297	Pumlumon Fach (Pumlumon Fawr)	664	2178

Notes 1. English name is Plynlimon, also named Pen Pumlumon Fawr
       2. Source of River Severn 2km to the north of the summit
       3. Top named by Bridge. Source of River Wye
          to the west of the summit

27. Rhayader

Sep Mtn	Top No	Name	Height in Metres	Feet
212	338	Drygarn Fawr	645	2116
252	422	Gorllwyn	613	2011
257	432	Pen y Garn	610	2001

Grid Ref	Ordnance Map 1/50k	1/25k	
789869	135	927	1.
815878	135/136	928	2.
799872	135/136	927	3.
776851	135	927	
787874	135	927	

Grid Ref	Ordnance Map 1/50k	1/25k
863584	147	991
918591	147	991
798771	135/147	947

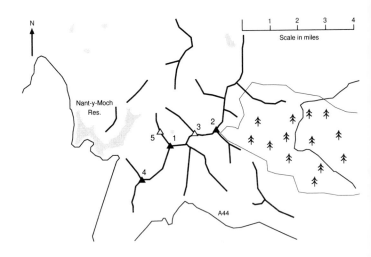

Map of the Pumlumon Group

1. Pumlumon Fawr
2. Pen Pumlumon Arwystli
3. Pen Pumlumon Llygad-bychan
4. Y Garn
5. Pumlumon Fach

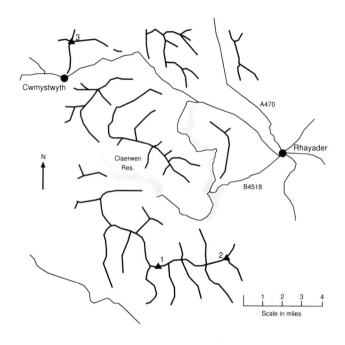

Map of the Rhayader Group

1. Drygarn Fawr
2. Gorllwyn
3. Pen y Garn

28. Radnor Forest

Sep Mtn	Top No	Name	Height in Metres	Feet
194	307	Great Rhos	660	2165
206	329	Black Mixen	650	2132
255	430	Bache Hill	610	2001

29. Black Mountains

Sep Mtn	Top No	Name	Height in Metres	Feet
56	81	Waun Fach	811	2660
65	92	Pen y Gadair Fawr	800	2624
117	182	Pen Allt-mawr	719	2358
-	192	Rhos Dirion (Waun Fach)	713	2339
134	209	Black Mountain	703	2306
138	216	Pen Cerrig-calch	701	2299
148	235	Twmpa	690	2263
159	256	Chwarel y Fan	679	2227
188	300	Mynydd Llysiau	663	2175
-	315	Pen Twyn-mawr (Pen y Gadair Fawr)	658	2158
-	336	Pen Twyn Glas (Pen Allt-mawr)	646	2119
-	350	Black Mountain - South Top (Black Mt'n)	637	2089

Notes 1. Also Pen y Gader Fawr
       2. Hereford and Worcester county top
       3. Also named The Tumpa or Lord Hereford's Knob
       4. Gwent county top

Grid Ref	Ordnance Map 1/50k	1/25k	
182639	148	970	
197644	148	970	
214636	137/148	971	

Grid Ref	Ordnance Map 1/50k	1/25k	
216300	161	13	
229288	161	13	1.
207243	161	13	
212334	161	13	
255355	161	13	2.
217224	161	13	
225351	161	13	3.
258294	161	13	4.
208279	161	13	
242267	161	13	
213257	161	13	
267322	161	13	

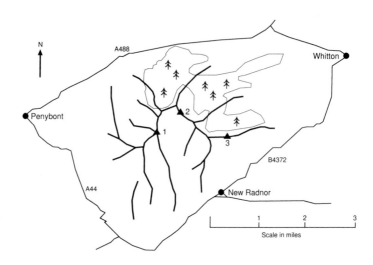

Map of the Radnor Forest Group

1. Great Rhos
2. Black Mixen
3. Bache Hill

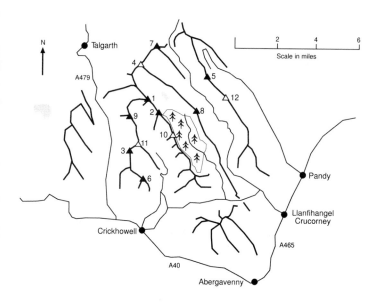

Map of the Black Mountain Group

1. Waun Fach
2. Pen y Gadair Fawr
3. Pen Allt Mawr
4. Rhos Dirion
5. Black Mountain
6. Pen Cerrig-calch

7. Twmpa
8. Chwarel y Fan
9. Mynydd Llysiau
10. Pen Twyn-mawr
11. Pen Twyn Glas
12. Black Mountain - South Top

30. Brecon Beacons

Sep Mtn	Top No	Name	Height in Metres	Feet
28	35	Pen y Fan	886	2906
-	39	Corn Du (Pen y Fan)	873	2864
60	86	Fan Brycheiniog	802	2631
68	96	Cribin	795	2608
85	126	Waun Rydd	769	2522
-	133	Fan Hir (Fan Brycheiniog)	761	2496
-	140	Bwlch y Ddwyallt (Waun Rydd)	754	2473
96	145	Picws Du	749	2457
107	164	Fan Fawr	734	2408
113	175	Fan Gyhirych	725	2378
-	181	Fan y Big (Waun Rydd)	719	2358
-	288	Fan Fraith (Fan Gyhirych)	668	2191
187	299	Fan Nedd	663	2175
201	321	Allt Lwyd	654	2145
218	357	Garreg Las	635	2083
223	366	Fan Llia	632	2073
-	372	Craig Cerrig-glesiad (Fan Fawr)	629	2063
225	373	Fan Frynych	629	2063
-	404	Y Gyrn (Corn Du)	619	2030
244	407	Cefn yr Ystrad	617	2024
246	410	Garreg-lwyd	616	2020

Notes 1. Powys county top
2. Also named Bannau Brycheiniog or Camarthen Fan
3. Spelt Waen-rydd on early OS maps
4. Also named Bannau Sir Gaer

Grid Ref	Ordnance Map 1/50k	1/25k	
012216	160	11	1.
007214	160	11	
825218	160	12	2.
024213	160	11	
062206	160	11	3.
831209	160	12	
055203	160	11	
812218	160	12	4.
970194	160	11	
881191	160	11	
036207	160	11	
887183	160	11	
913184	160	11	
079189	160	11	
777203	160	12	5.
938186	160	11	
961218	160	11	6.
958228	160	11	
989216	160	11	
087137	160	11	7.
740179	160	12	8.

5. Summit is named Carnau'r Gerreg Las
6. Also named Rhos Dringarth
7. Summit is named Carn Felan, also Mynydd Llangynidir
8. Also named Moel Gornach

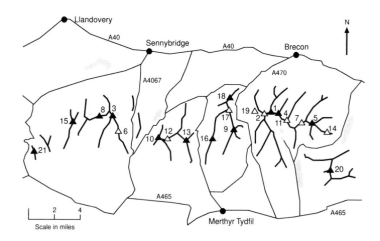

Map of the Brecon Beacons Group

1. Pen y Fan
2. Corn Du
3. Fan Brycheiniog
4. Cribin
5. Waun Rydd
6. Fan Hir
7. Bwlch y Ddyallt
8. Picws Du
9. Fan Fawr
10. Fan Gyhirych
11. Fan y Big
12. Fan Fraith
13. Fan Nedd
14. Allt Lwyd
15. Garreg Las
16. Fan Llia
17. Craig Cerrig-glesiad
18. Fan Frynych
19. Y Gyrn
20. Cefn yr Ystrad
21. Garreg-lwyd

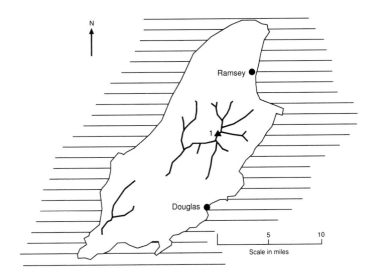

Map of the Isle of Man Group

1. Snaefell

31. Isle of Man

Sep Mtn	Top No	Name	Height in Metres	Feet
238	396	Snaefell	621	2037

Grid Ref	Ordnance Map	
	1/50k	1/25k
398881	95	-

TABLE OF THE 2000-FOOT MOUNTAINS OF ENGLAND AND WALES IN ORDER OF
ALTITUDE

Sep Mtn	Top No	Name	Group
1	1	Yr Wyddfa	Snowdon
2	2	Crib y Ddysgl	Snowdon
3	3	Carnedd Llywelyn	Carneddau
4	4	Carnedd Dafydd	Carneddau
5	5	Glyder Fawr	Glyders
6	6	Glyder Fach	Glyders
7	7	Pen yr Ole Wen	Carneddau
8	8	Scafell Pike	Scafell
9	9	Foel-grach	Carneddau
10	10	Sca Fell	Scafell
11	11	Yr Elen	Carneddau
-	12	Symonds Knott	Scafell
12	13	Helvellyn	Helvellyn
13	14	Y Garn	Glyders
14	15	Foel-fras	Carneddau
-	16	Ill Crag	Scafell
-	17	Broad Crag	Scafell
15	18	Skiddaw	Skiddaw
-	19	Garnedd Uchaf	Carneddau
-	20	Lower Man	Helvellyn
16	21	Elidir Fawr	Glyders
17	22	Crib-goch	Snowdon
18	23	Tryfan	Glyders
19	24	Great End	Scafell
20	25	Aran Fawddwy	Arans
21	26	Bow Fell	Scafell
22	27	Great Gable	Great Gable
23	28	Y Lliwedd	Snowdon
24	29	Cross Fell	Cross Fell
25	30	Cadair Idris	Cadair Idris
-	31	Y Lliwedd - East Top	Snowdon

Height in in metres	Date Ascended/Notes
1085	_____
1065	_____
1064	_____
1044	_____
999	_____
994	_____
978	_____
978	_____
976	_____
964	_____
962	_____
959	_____
950	_____
947	_____
942	_____
935	_____
934	_____
931	_____
926	_____
925	_____
924	_____
923	_____
915	_____
910	_____
905	_____
902	_____
899	_____
898	_____
893	_____
893	_____
893	_____

Sep Mtn	Top No	Name	Group
26	32	Pillar	Great Gable
-	33	Nethermost Pike	Helvellyn
27	34	Catstye Cam	Helvellyn
28	35	Pen y Fan	Brecon Beacons
29	36	Aran Benllyn	Arans
30	37	Esk Pike	Scafell
31	38	Raise	Helvellyn
-	39	Corn Du	Brecon Beacons
32	40	Fairfield	Helvellyn
-	41	Erw y Ddafad-ddu	Arans
33	42	Moel Siabod	Moelwyns
34	43	Blencathra	Skiddaw
-	44	Bowfell - North Top	Scafell
35	45	Little Man	Skiddaw
36	46	Mynydd Moel	Cadair Idris
-	47	White Side	Helvellyn
-	48	Striding Edge	Helvellyn
37	49	Crinkle Crags	Scafell
38	50	Dollywaggon Pike	Helvellyn
39	51	Great Dodd	Helvellyn
40	52	Arenig Fawr	Arenigs
41	53	Grasmoor	Buttermere
-	54	Gategill Fell Top	Skiddaw
-	55	Llwytmor	Carneddau
42	56	Great Dun Fell	Cross Fell
-	57	Atkinson Pike	Skiddaw
43	58	Stybarrow Dodd	Helvellyn
44	59	Little Dun Fell	Cross Fell
45	60	Little Scoat Fell	Great Gable
46	61	St Sunday Crag	Helvellyn
47	62	Crag Hill	Buttermere
-	63	Pen y Diocyn	Arenigs
-	64	Flesk	Scafell
48	65	Pen yr Helgi-du	Carneddau

Height in in metres	Date Ascended/Notes
892	_____
891	_____
890	_____
886	_____
885	_____
885	_____
883	_____
873	_____
873	_____
872	_____
872	_____
868	_____
866	_____
865	_____
863	_____
863	_____
860+	_____
859	_____
858	_____
857	_____
854	_____
852	_____
851	_____
849	_____
848	_____
845	_____
843	_____
842	_____
841	_____
841	_____
839	_____
836	_____
834	_____
833	_____

Sep Mtn	Top No	Name	Group
49	66	Foel-goch	Glyders
50	67	Cadair Berwyn - South Top	Berwyns
-	68	Black Crag	Great Gable
51	69	High Street	High Street
-	70	Cadair Berwyn	Berwyns
-	71	Moel Sych	Berwyns
52	72	Red Pike - Wasdale	Great Gable
53	73	Hart Crag	Helvellyn
54	74	Carnedd y Filiast	Glyders
-	75	Steeple	Great Gable
-	76	Lliwedd Bach	Snowdon
55	77	The Cheviot	Cheviot
-	78	Shelter Crags	Scafell
-	79	Mynydd Perfedd	Glyders
-	80	Cyfrwy	Cadair Idris
56	81	Waun Fach	Black Mountains
-	82	Bera Bach	Carneddau
57	83	High Stile	Great Gable
58	84	Y Foel-goch	Glyders
59	85	The Old Man of Coniston	Coniston
60	86	Fan Brycheiniog	Brecon Beacons
61	87	High Raise	High Street
62	88	Kirk Fell	Great Gable
63	89	Swirl How	Coniston
-	90	Green Gable	Great Gable
64	91	Lingmell	Scafell
65	92	Pen y Gadair Fawr	Black Mountains
66	93	Pen Llithrig-y-wrach	Carneddau
67	94	Haycock	Great Gable
-	95	Brim Fell	Coniston
68	96	Cribin	Brecon Beacons
-	97	Green Side	Helvellyn
-	98	Bera Mawr	Carneddau
69	99	Knock Fell	Cross Fell

Height in in metres	Date Ascended/Notes
831	_____
830	_____
828	_____
828	_____
827	_____
827	_____
826	_____
822	_____
821	_____
819	_____
818	_____
815	_____
815	_____
812	_____
811	_____
811	_____
807	_____
807	_____
805	_____
803	_____
802	_____
802	_____
802	_____
802	_____
801	_____
800+	_____
800	_____
799	_____
797	_____
796	_____
795	_____
795	_____
794	_____
794	_____

Sep Mtn	Top No	Name	Group
-	100	Dove Crag	Helvellyn
-	101	Rampsgill Head	High Street
70	102	Craig Cwm Amarch	Cadair Idris
71	103	Grisedale Pike	Buttermere
72	104	Mickle Fell	Cross Fell
-	105	Kirk Fell - East Top	Great Gable
73	106	Allan Crag	Scafell
-	107	Great Carrs	Coniston
74	108	Cadair Bronwen	Berwyns
-	109	Thornthwaite Crag	High Street
75	110	Glaramara	Scafell
76	111	Moel Hebog	Moel Hebog
-	112	Kidsty Pike	High Street
-	113	Pillar Rock	Great Gable
77	114	Glasgwm	Arans
78	115	Dow Crag	Coniston
79	116	Harter Fell	High Street
80	117	Red Screes	Helvellyn
-	118	Looking Steads	Scafell
-	119	Shelter Crags - North Top	Scafell
-	120	Sail	Buttermere
-	121	Wandope	Buttermere
81	122	Grey Friar	Coniston
82	123	Drum	Carneddau
83	124	Hopegill Head	Buttermere
84	125	Moelwyn Mawr	Moelwyns
85	126	Waun Rydd	Brecon Beacons
86	127	Meldon Hill	Cross Fell
-	128	Great Rigg	Helvellyn
-	129	Gallt yr Ogof	Glyders
87	130	Stony Cove Pike	High Street
88	131	High Raise	Scafell
89	132	Wetherlam	Coniston
-	133	Fan Hir	Brecon Beacons

Height in in metres	Date Ascended/Notes
792	_____
792	_____
791	_____
791	_____
788	_____
787	_____
785	_____
785	_____
784	_____
784	_____
783	_____
782	_____
780+	_____
780	_____
779	_____
778	_____
778	_____
776	_____
775	_____
775	_____
773	_____
772	_____
770+	_____
770	_____
770	_____
770	_____
769	_____
767	_____
766	_____
763	_____
763	_____
762	_____
762	_____
761	_____

Sep Mtn	Top No	Name	Group
-	134	Drosgl	Carneddau
90	135	Ill Bell	High Street
-	136	Hart Side	Helvellyn
-	137	Sand Hill	Buttermere
91	138	Y Llethr	Rhinogs
-	139	Red Pike - Buttermere	Great Gable
-	140	Bwlch y Ddwyallt	Brecon Beacons
92	141	Dale Head	Buttermere
93	142	Pumlumon Fawr	Pumlumon
94	143	Moel Llyfnant	Arenigs
95	144	Diffwys	Rhinogs
96	145	Picws Du	Brecon Beacons
97	146	Burnhope Seat	Burnhope Seat
98	147	Yr Aran	Snowdon
-	148	Carl Side	Skiddaw
-	149	Black Sails	Coniston
99	150	Little Fell	Cross Fell
100	151	High Crag	Great Gable
101	152	Pen Pumlumon Arwystli	Pumlumon
-	153	Round How	Scafell
-	154	Tomle	Berwyns
-	155	Little Stand	Scafell
-	156	Hobcarton Crag	Buttermere
102	157	Robinson	Buttermere
103	158	Harrison Stickle	Scafell
104	159	Seat Sandal	Helvellyn
105	160	Whernside	Ingleborough
-	161	Combe Head	Scafell
-	162	Craig Eigiau	Carneddau
106	163	Craig Cwm Silyn	Moel Hebog
107	164	Fan Fawr	Brecon Beacons
-	165	Long Side	Skiddaw
108	166	Rhobell Fawr	Arenigs
-	167	Little Gowder Crag	Great Gable

Height in in metres	*Date Ascended/Notes*
758	_____
757	_____
756	_____
756	_____
756	_____
755	_____
754	_____
753	_____
752	_____
751	_____
750	_____
749	_____
747	_____
747	_____
746	_____
745	_____
745	_____
744	_____
741	_____
741	_____
741	_____
740	_____
739	_____
737	_____
736	_____
736	_____
736	_____
735	_____
735	_____
734	_____
734	_____
734	_____
734	_____
733	_____

Sep Mtn	Top No	Name	Group
-	168	Codale Head	Scafell
-	169	Kentmere Pike	High Street
109	170	Hindscarth	Buttermere
-	171	Pen Pumlumon Llygad-bychan	Pumlumon
110	172	Clough Head	Helvellyn
111	173	Moel Eilio	Snowdon
112	174	Ullscarf	Scafell
113	175	Fan Gihirych	Brecon Beacons
114	176	Ingleborough	Ingleborough
-	177	Thunacar Knott	Scafell
-	178	Red Beck Top	Scafell
115	179	Froswick	High Street
116	180	Rhinog Fawr	Rhinogs
-	181	Fan y Big	Brecon Beacons
117	182	Pen Allt-mawr	Black Mountains
-	183	Whiteside - East Top	Buttermere
-	184	Birkhouse Moor	Helvellyn
-	185	Llechog	Snowdon
-	186	Redgleam	Burnhope Seat
118	187	Great Shunner Fell	Great Shunner
119	188	Brandreth	Great Gable
120	189	Lonscale Fell	Skiddaw
121	190	Hedgehope Hill	Cheviots
122	191	Branstree	High Street
-	192	Rhos Dirion	Black Mountains
-	193	Moel Merddwr	Arenigs
123	194	Rhinog Fach	Rhinogs
124	195	Dead Stones	Burnhope Seat
-	196	Gray Crag	High Street
125	197	Knott	Skiddaw
126	198	Moelwyn Bach	Moelwyns
127	199	High Seat	Great Shunner
128	200	Melmerby Fell	Cross Fell
-	201	Pike of Stickle	Scafell

Height in in metres	Date Ascended/Notes
730+	_____
730	_____
727	_____
727	_____
726	_____
726	_____
726	_____
725	_____
723	_____
723	_____
721	_____
720	_____
720	_____
719	_____
719	_____
719	_____
718	_____
718	_____
718	_____
716	_____
715	_____
715	_____
714	_____
713	_____
713	_____
712	_____
712	_____
710+	_____
710	_____
710	_____
710	_____
709	_____
709	_____
709	_____

Sep Mtn	Top No	Name	Group
129	202	Trum y Ddysgl	Moel Hebog
130	203	High Field	Burnhope Seat
131	204	Wild Boar Fell	Great Shunner
-	205	Whiteside	Buttermere
-	206	Yoke	High Street
132	207	Pike of Blisco	Scafell
133	208	Great Whernside	Ingleborough
134	209	Black Mountain	Black Mountains
135	210	Chapelfell Top	Burnhope Seat
-	211	Ladyside Pike	Buttermere
-	212	Middleboot Knotts	Scafell
136	213	Bowscale Fell	Skiddaw
137	214	Buckden Pike	Ingleborough
-	215	Cold Pike	Scafell
138	216	Pen Cerrig-calch	Black Mountains
-	217	Pavey Ark	Scafell
-	218	Garnedd Goch	Moel Hebog
-	219	Pen-y-bryn	Berwyns
139	220	Backstone Edge	Cross Fell
140	221	Allt-fawr	Moelwyns
141	222	Mynydd Mawr	Moel Hebog
-	223	Grey Knotts	Great Gable
-	224	Fendrith Hill	Burnhope Seat
-	225	Great Knott	Scafell
142	226	Rest Dodd	High Street
-	227	Moel yr Ewig	Berwyns
143	228	Mynydd Drws-y-coed	Moel Hebog
-	229	Archy Stryrigg	Great Shunner
144	230	Pen-y-gent	Ingleborough
145	231	Seatallan	Great Gable
-	232	Caw Fell	Great Gable
146	233	Foel Wen	Berwyns
147	234	Great Calva	Skiddaw
148	235	Twmpa	Black Mountains

Height in in metres	Date Ascended/Notes
709	_____
708	_____
708	_____
707	_____
706	_____
705	_____
704	_____
703	_____
703	_____
703	_____
703	_____
702	_____
702	_____
701	_____
701	_____
700+	_____
700	_____
700	_____
699	_____
698	_____
698	_____
697	_____
696	_____
696	_____
696	_____
695	_____
695	_____
695	_____
694	_____
692	_____
690+	_____
690	_____
690	_____
690	_____

Sep Mtn	Top No	Name	Group
149	236	Arenig Fach	Arenigs
150	237	Cnicht	Moelwyns
-	238	Craigysgafn	Moelwyns
151	239	Foel Hafod-fynydd	Arans
-	240	Hugh Seat	Great Shunner
-	241	Carnedd y Ddelw	Carneddau
-	242	Foel Wen - South Top	Berwyns
152	243	Great Coum	Ingleborough
153	244	Round Hill	Cross Fell
-	245	Gwaun y Llwyni	Arans
154	246	Pen y Bryn-fforchog	Arans
-	247	High House Tarn Top	Scafell
155	248	Y Garn	Pumlumon
156	249	Bannerdale Crags	Skiddaw
-	250	Cold Pike - West Top	Scafell
-	251	Gau Graig	Cadair Idris
-	252	Mynydd Tarw	Berwyns
157	253	Swarth Fell	Great Shunner
-	254	Loft Crag	Scafell
158	255	Plover Hill	Ingleborough
159	256	Chwarel y Fan	Black Mountains
-	257	Godor	Berwyns
160	258	Cregiau Gleision	Carneddau
161	259	Tarn Rigg Hill	Great Shunner
162	260	The Calf	Great Shunner
-	261	Combe Door	Scafell
-	262	Knoutberry Haw	Great Shunner
163	263	Moel Druman	Moelwyns
-	264	Godor - North Top	Berwyns
164	265	James's Hill	Burnhope Seat
165	266	Lovely Seat	Great Shunner
166	267	Maesglase	Cadair Idris
167	268	Murton Fell	Cross Fell
168	269	Sheffield Pike	Helvellyn

Height in in metres	*Date Ascended/Notes*
689	_____
689	_____
689	_____
689	_____
689	_____
688	_____
687	_____
687	_____
686	_____
685	_____
685	_____
684	_____
684	_____
683	_____
683	_____
683	_____
681	_____
681	_____
680+	_____
680+	_____
679	_____
679	_____
678	_____
678	_____
676	_____
676	_____
676	_____
676	_____
675	_____
675	_____
675	_____
675	_____
675	_____
675	_____

Sep Mtn	Top No	Name	Group
-	270	Calders	Great Shunner
169	271	Moel Cynghorion	Snowdon
170	272	Killhope Law	Burnhope Seat
-	273	Nowtli Hill	High Street
-	274	Bram Rigg Top	Great Shunner
171	275	Great Knoutberry Hill	Ingleborough
172	276	Rogan's Seat	Great Shunner
173	277	Scar Crags	Buttermere
-	278	Ysgafell Wen	Moelwyns
174	279	Esgeiriau Gwynion	Arans
175	280	Loadpot Hill	High Street
-	281	Cold Pike - Far West Top	Scafell
-	282	Crib-y-rhiw	Rhinogs
176	283	Wether Hill	High Street
177	284	Waun-oer	Cadair Idris
178	285	Carnedd y Filiast	Arenigs
-	286	Ysgafell Wen - North Top	Moelwyns
179	287	Dodd Fell Hill	Ingleborough
-	288	Fan Fraith	Brecon Beacons
180	289	Fountains Fell	Ingleborough
-	290	Water Crag	Great Shunner
181	291	Cyrniau Nod	Berwyns
182	292	Tarren y Gesail	Cadair Idris
183	293	Sails	Great Shunner
-	294	Sale How	Skiddaw
184	295	Post Gwyn	Berwyns
185	296	Black Fell	Black Fell
-	297	Pumlumon Fach	Pumlumon
186	298	Tarn Crag	High Street
187	299	Fan Nedd	Brecon Beacons
188	300	Mynydd Llysiau	Black Mountains
-	301	Fountains Fell - South Top	Ingleborough
189	302	Nine Standards Rigg	Great Shunner
190	303	Manod Mawr	Moelwyns

Height in in metres	Date Ascended/Notes
674	_____
674	_____
673	_____
673	_____
672	_____
672	_____
672	_____
672	_____
672	_____
671	_____
671	_____
670+	_____
670+	_____
670+	_____
670	_____
669	_____
669	_____
668	_____
668	_____
668	_____
668	_____
667	_____
667	_____
667	_____
666	_____
665	_____
664	_____
664	_____
664	_____
663	_____
663	_____
662	_____
662	_____
661	_____

Sep Mtn	Top No	Name	Group
191	304	Tyrau Mawr	Cadair Idris
192	305	Carrock Fell	Skiddaw
193	306	Dduallt	Arenigs
194	307	Great Rhos	Radnor Forest
-	308	Whiteless Pike	Buttermere
195	309	Cribin Fawr	Cadair Idris
-	310	Foel Rhudd	Arans
-	311	Y Groes Fagl	Berwyns
196	312	High Pike	Skiddaw
-	313	Long Man Hill	Cross Fell
197	314	Manod Mawr - North Top	Moelwyns
-	315	Pen Twyn-mawr	Black Mountains
198	316	Place Fell	High Street
-	317	Coldbarrow Fell	Scafell
199	318	Grey Nag	Black Fell
200	319	Moel yr Ogof	Moel Hebog
-	320	Selside	High Street
201	321	Allt Lwyd	Brecon Beacons
202	322	Harter Fell	Coniston
203	323	High Spy	Buttermere
-	324	Mynydd Tal-y-mignedd	Moel Hebog
204	325	Comb Fell	Cheviots
-	326	Rossett Pike	Scafell
205	327	Three Pikes	Burnhope Seat
-	328	Ysgafell Wen - Far North Top	Moelwyns
206	329	Black Mixen	Radnor Forest
-	330	Simon Fell	Ingleborough
207	331	Viewing Hill	Cross Fell
208	332	Fleetwith Pike	Great Gable
209	333	Foel Cwm Sian-llwyd	Berwyns
210	334	Moel-yr-hydd	Moelwyns
-	335	Base Brown	Great Gable
-	336	Pen Twyn Glas	Black Mountains
211	337	Pen y Boncyn Trefeilw	Berwyns

Height in in metres	Date Ascended/Notes
661	_____
660+	_____
660+	_____
660	_____
660	_____
659	_____
659	_____
659	_____
658	_____
658	_____
658	_____
658	_____
657	_____
656	_____
656	_____
655	_____
655	_____
654	_____
653	_____
653	_____
653	_____
652	_____
651	_____
651	_____
650+	_____
650	_____
650	_____
649	_____
648	_____
648	_____
648	_____
646	_____
646	_____
646	_____

Sep Mtn	Top No	Name	Group
212	338	Drygarn Fawr	Rhayader
-	339	Gyrn Wigau	Carneddau
-	340	Carnedd Llechwedd-llyfn	Arenigs
213	341	Yockenthwaite Moor	Ingleborough
-	342	Craig Bodlyn	Rhinogs
-	343	Little Calva	Skiddaw
-	344	Dodd	Great Gable
214	345	Fell Head	Great Shunner
215	346	Iron Crag	Great Gable
216	347	Yarlside	Great Shunner
-	348	Grey Crag	High Street
-	349	Moel Lefn	Moel Hebog
-	350	Black Mountain - South Top	Black Mountains
-	351	Causey Pike	Buttermere
-	352	Dovenest Top	Scafell
-	353	Harrop Pike	High Street
-	354	Little Hart Crag	Helvellyn
-	355	Tom Smith's Stone Top	Black Fell
217	356	Kinder Scout	Peak District
218	357	Garreg Las	Brecon Beacons
-	358	Blea Crag	Buttermere
219	359	Fiend's Fell	Cross Fell
-	360	Hobcarton End	Buttermere
-	361	Pen Cowlyd	Carneddau
220	362	Tarrenhendre	Cadair Idris
221	363	Bleaklow	Peak District
222	364	Starling Dodd	Great Gable
-	365	Y Garn	Moel Hebog
223	366	Fan Llia	Brecon Beacons
-	367	Gwaun Lydan	Arans
-	368	Seathwaite Fell	Scafell
-	369	Seathwaite Fell - South Top	Scafell
-	370	Stack Rhos	Berwyns
224	371	Moel Fferna	Berwyns

Height in in metres	Date Ascended/Notes
645	_____
643	_____
643	_____
643	_____
642	_____
642	_____
641	_____
640+	_____
640+	_____
639	_____
638	_____
638	_____
637	_____
637	_____
637	_____
637	_____
637	_____
637	_____
636	_____
635	_____
634	_____
634	_____
634	_____
634	_____
634	_____
633	_____
633	_____
633	_____
632	_____
632	_____
632	_____
631	_____
630+	_____
630	_____

Sep Mtn	Top No	Name	Group
-	372	Craig Cerrig Glesiad	Brecon Beacons
225	373	Fan Frynych	Brecon Beacons
-	374	Foel-gron	Snowdon
226	375	Y Garn	Rhinogs
-	376	Green Hill	Ingleborough
-	377	Rough Crag	High Street
227	378	Yewbarrow	Great Gable
228	379	Gragareth	Ingleborough
-	380	Hare Stones	Skiddaw
-	381	Looking Stead	Great Gable
229	382	Foel y Geifr	Arans
230	383	Moel y Cerrig-duon	Arans
231	384	Darnbrook Fell	Ingleborough
232	385	Randygill Top	Great Shunner
-	386	Bush Howe	Great Shunner
233	387	Moel Ysgyfarnogod	Rhinogs
-	388	Pen y Castell	Carneddau
-	389	Birks	Helvellyn
234	390	Craig y Llyn	Cadair Idris
235	391	Cold Fell	Black Fell
-	392	Erne Crag	Helvellyn
-	393	Higher Shelf Stones	Peak District
236	394	High Willhays	Dartmoor
237	395	Pen Bwlch Llandrillo Top	Berwyns
238	396	Snaefell	Isle of Man
-	397	Walna Scar	Coniston
239	398	Bellbeaver Rigg	Cross Fell
240	399	Pen yr Allt-uchaf	Arans
241	400	Bink Moss	Cross Fell
242	401	Gallt y Daren	Arenigs
-	402	Gallt y Wenallt	Snowdon
243	403	Windy Gyle	Cheviots
-	404	Y Gyrn	Brecon Beacons
-	405	Yes Tor	Dartmoor

Height in in metres	Date Ascended/Notes
629	_____
629	_____
629	_____
629	_____
628	_____
628	_____
628	_____
627	_____
627	_____
627	_____
626	_____
625	_____
624	_____
624	_____
623	_____
623	_____
623	_____
622	_____
622	_____
621	_____
621	_____
621	_____
621	_____
621	_____
621	_____
621	_____
620+	_____
620+	_____
619	_____
619	_____
619	_____
619	_____
619	_____
619	_____

Sep Mtn	Top No	Name	Group
-	406	Hartsop Dodd	High Street
244	407	Cefn yr Ystrad	Brecon Beacons
245	408	Cushat Law	Cheviots
-	409	Foel Boeth	Arenigs
246	410	Garreg-lwyd	Brecon Beacons
247	411	Great Borne	Great Gable
-	412	Great Lingy Hill	Skiddaw
-	413	Stirrup Crag	Great Gable
-	414	Cefn Gwyntog	Berwyns
248	415	The Dodd	Burnhope Seat
249	416	Drumaldrace	Ingleborough
250	417	Flinty Fell	Burnhope Seat
-	418	Foel Penolau	Rhinogs
-	419	Llechwedd Du	Arans
251	420	Moel Penamnen	Moelwyns
-	421	Foel Goch	Arans
252	422	Gorllwyn	Rhayader
253	423	Burtree Fell	Burnhope Seat
-	424	Heron Pike	Helvellyn
-	425	Rosthwaite Cam	Scafell
-	426	Trum y Gwrgedd	Arans
254	427	Foel Goch	Arenigs
-	428	Bullman Hills	Cross Fell
-	429	White Maiden	Coniston
255	430	Bache Hill	Radnor Forest
256	431	Bloodybush Edge	Cheviots
257	432	Pen y Garn	Rhayader
258	433	Tal y Fan	Carneddau

Height in in metres	Date Ascended/Notes
618	_____
617	_____
616	_____
616	_____
616	_____
616	_____
616	_____
616	_____
615	_____
614	_____
614	_____
614	_____
614	_____
614	_____
614	_____
613	_____
613	_____
612	_____
612	_____
612	_____
612	_____
611	_____
610+	_____
610+	_____
610	_____
610	_____
610	_____
610	_____

TABLE OF THE 2000-FOOT MOUNTAINS OF ENGLAND AND WALES IN
ALPHABETICAL ORDER

Name	Top No
Allan Crags	106
Allt-fawr	221
Allt Lwyd	321
Aran Benllyn	36
Aran Fawddwy	25
Archy Stryrigg	229
Arenig Fach	236
Arenig Fawr	52
Atkinson Pike	57
Bache Hill	430
Backstone Edge	220
Bannerdale Crags	249
Base Brown	335
Bellbeaver Rigg	398
Bera Bach	82
Bera Mawr	98
Bink Moss	400
Birkhouse Moor	184
Birks	389
Black Crag	68
Black Fell	296
Black Mixen	329
Black Mountain	209
Black Mountain - South Top	350
Black Sails	149
Blea Crag	358
Bleaklow	363
Blencathra	43
Bloodybush Edge	431
Bow Fell	26
Bowfell - North Top	44

Name	Top No
Bowscale Fell	213
Bram Rigg Top	274
Brandreth	188
Branstree	191
Brim Fell	95
Broad Crag	17
Buckden Pike	214
Bullman Hills	428
Burnhope Seat	146
Burtree Fell	423
Bush Howe	386
Bwlch y Ddwyallt	140
Cadair Berwyn	70
Cadair Berwyn - South Top	67
Cadair Bronwen	108
Cadair Idris	30
Calder	270
Calf The	260
Carl Side	148
Carnedd Dafydd	4
Carnedd Llechwedd-llyfn	340
Carnedd Llywelyn	3
Carnedd y Ddelw	241
Carnedd y Filiast (Arenigs)	285
Carnedd y Filiast (Glyders)	74
Carrock Fell	305
Catstye Cam	34
Causey Pike	351
Caw Fell	232
Cefn Gwyntog	414
Cefn yr Ystrad	407
Chapelfell Top	210
Cheviot The	77
Chwarel y Fan	256

Name	*Top No*
Clough Head	172
Cnicht	237
Codale Head	168
Cold Fell	391
Cold Pike	215
Cold Pike - Far West Top	281
Cold Pike - West Top	250
Coldbarrow Fell	317
Comb Fell	325
Combe Door	261
Combe Head	161
Corn Du	39
Crag Hill	62
Craig Bodlyn	342
Craig Cerrig-glesiad	372
Craig Cwm Amarch	102
Craig Cwm Silyn	163
Craig Eigiau	162
Craig y Llyn	390
Craigysgafn	238
Cregiau Gleision	258
Crib y Ddysgl	2
Crib-y-rhiw	282
Cribin	96
Cribin Fawr	309
Crib-goch	22
Crinkle Crags	49
Cross Fell	29
Cushat Law	408
Cyfrwy	80
Cyrniau Nod	291
Dale Head	141
Darnbrook Fell	384
Dduallt	306

Name	*Top No*
Dead Stones	195
Diffwys	144
Dodd Fell Hill	287
Dodd The	415
Dodd	344
Dollywaggon	50
Dove Crag	100
Dovenest Top	352
Dow Crag	115
Drosgl	134
Drum	123
Drumaldrace	416
Drygarn Fawr	338
Elidir Fawr	21
Erne Crag	392
Erw y Ddafad-ddu	41
Esgeiriau Gwynion	279
Esk Pike	37
Fairfield	40
Fan Brycheiniog	86
Fan Fawr	164
Fan Fraith	288
Fan Frynych	373
Fan Gyhirych	175
Fan Hir	133
Fan Llia	366
Fan Nedd	299
Fan y Big	181
Fell Head	345
Fendrith Hill	224
Fiend's Fell	359
Fleetwith Pike	332
Flesk	64
Flinty Fell	417

Name	Top No
Foel Boeth	409
Foel Cwm Sian-llwyd	333
Foel Goch (Arans)	421
Foel Goch (Arenigs)	427
Foel Hafod-fynydd	239
Foel Penolau	418
Foel Rhudd	310
Foel Wen	233
Foel Wen - South Top	242
Foel y Geifr	382
Foel-fras	15
Foel-goch	66
Foel-grach	9
Foel-gron	374
Fountains Fell	289
Fountains Fell - South Top	301
Froswick	179
Gallt y Daren	401
Gallt y Wenallt	402
Gallt yr Ogof	129
Garnedd Goch	218
Garnedd Uchaf	19
Garreg Las	357
Garreg-lwyd	410
Gategill Fell Top	54
Gau Graig	251
Glaramara	110
Glasgwm	114
Glyder Fach	6
Glyder Fawr	5
Godor	257
Godor - North Top	264
Gorllwyn	422
Gragareth	379

Name	*Top No*
Grasmoor	53
Gray Crag	196
Great Borne	411
Great Calva	234
Great Carrs	107
Great Coum	243
Great Dodd	51
Great Dun Fell	56
Great End	24
Great Gable	27
Great Knott	225
Great Knoutberry Hill	275
Great Lingy Hill	412
Great Rhos	307
Great Rigg	128
Great Shunner Fell	187
Great Whernside	208
Green Gable	90
Green Hill	376
Green Side	97
Grey Crag	348
Grey Friar	122
Grey Knotts	223
Grey Nag	318
Grisedale Pike	103
Gwaun Lydan	367
Gwaun y Llwyni	245
Gyrn Wigau	339
Hare Stones	380
Harrison Stickle	158
Harrop Pike	353
Hart Crag	73
Hart Side	136
Harter Fell (High Street)	116

Name	Top No
Harter Fell (Scafell)	322
Hartsop Dodd	406
Haycock	94
Hedgehope Hill	190
Helvellyn	13
Heron Pike	424
High Crag	151
High Field	203
High House Tarn Top	247
High Pike	312
High Raise (High Street)	87
High Raise (Scafell)	131
High Seat	199
High Spy	323
High Stile	83
High Street	69
High Willhays	394
Higher Shelf Stones	393
Hindscarth	170
Hobcarton Crag	156
Hobcarton End	360
Hopegill Head	124
Hugh Seat	240
Ill Bell	135
Ill Crag	16
Ingleborough	176
Iron Crag	346
James's Hill	265
Kentmere Pike	169
Kidsty Pike	112
Killhope Law	272
Kinder Scout	356
Kirk Fell	88
Kirk Fell - East Top	105

Name	*Top No*
Knock Fell	99
Knott	197
Knoutberry Haw	262
Ladyside Pike	211
Lingmell	91
Little Calva	343
Little Dun Fell	59
Little Fell	150
Little Gowder Crag	167
Little Hart Crag	354
Little Man	45
Little Scoat Fell	60
Little Stand	155
Llechog	185
Llechwedd Du	419
Lliwedd Bach	76
Llwytmor	55
Loadpot Hill	280
Loft Crag	254
Long Man Hill	313
Long Side	165
Lonscale Fell	189
Looking Stead (Great Gable)	381
Looking Steads (Scafell)	118
Lovely Seat	266
Lower Man	20
Maesglase	267
Manod Mawr	303
Manod Mawr - North Top	314
Meldon Hill	127
Melmerby Fell	200
Mickle Fell	104
Middleboot Knotts	212
Moel Cynghorion	271

Name	Top No
Moel Druman	263
Moel Eilio	173
Moel Fferna	371
Moel Hebog	111
Moel Lefn	349
Moel Llyfnant	143
Moel Merddwr	193
Moel Penamnen	420
Moel Siabod	42
Moel Sych	71
Moel Ysgyfarnogod	387
Moel y Cerrig-duon	383
Moel yr Ewig	227
Moel yr Ogof	319
Moelwyn Bach	198
Moelwyn Mawr	125
Moel-yr-hydd	334
Murton Fell	268
Mynydd Drws-y-coed	228
Mynydd Llysiau	300
Mynydd Mawr	222
Mynydd Moel	46
Mynydd Perfedd	79
Mynydd Tal-y-mignedd	324
Mynydd Tarw	252
Nethermost Pike	33
Nine Standards Rigg	302
Nowtli Hill	273
Old Man of Coniston The	85
Pavey Ark	217
Pen Allt-mawr	182
Pen Bwlch Llandrillo Top	395
Pen Cerrig-calch	216
Pen Cowlyd	361

Name	Top No
Pen Llithrig-y-wrach	93
Pen Pumlumon Arwystli	152
Pen Pumlumon Llygad-bychan	171
Pen Twyn Glas	336
Pen Twyn-mawr	315
Pen y Boncyn Trefeilw	337
Pen y Bryn-fforchog	246
Pen y Castell	388
Pen y Diocyn	63
Pen y Fan	35
Pen y Gadair Fawr	92
Pen y Garn	432
Pen yr Allt-uchaf	399
Pen yr Helgi-du	65
Pen yr Ole Wen	7
Pen-y-bryn	219
Pen-y-gent	230
Picws Du	145
Pike of Blisco	207
Pike of Stickle	201
Pillar	32
Pillar Rock	113
Place Fell	316
Plover Hill	255
Post Gwyn	295
Pumlumon Fach	297
Pumlumon Fawr	142
Raise	38
Rampsgill Head	101
Randygill Top	385
Red Beck Top	178
Red Pike - Buttermere	139
Red Pike - Wasdale	72
Red Screes	117

Name	Top No
Redgleam	186
Rest Dodd	226
Rhinog Fach	194
Rhinog Fawr	180
Rhobell Fawr	166
Rhos Dirion	192
Robinson	157
Rogan's Seat	276
Rossett Pike	326
Rosthwaite Cam	425
Rough Crag	377
Round Hill	244
Round How	153
Sail	120
Sails	293
Sale How	294
Sand Hill	137
Sca Fell	10
Scafell Pike	8
Scar Crags	277
Seat Sandal	159
Seatallan	231
Seathwaite Fell	368
Seathwaite Fell - South Top	369
Selside	320
Sheffield Pike	269
Shelter Crags	78
Shelter Crags - North Top	119
Simon Fell	330
Skiddaw	18
Snaefell	396
St Sunday Crag	61
Stack Rhos	370
Starling Dodd	364

Name	Top No
Steeple	75
Stirrup Crag	413
Stony Cove Pike	130
Striding Edge	48
Stybarrow Dodd	58
Swarth Fell	253
Swirl How	89
Symonds Knott	12
Tal y Fan	433
Tarn Crag	298
Tarn Rigg Hill	259
Tarren y Gesail	292
Tarrenhendre	362
Thornthwaite Crag	109
Three Pikes	327
Thunacar Knott	177
Tom Smith's Stone Top	355
Tomle	154
Trum y Ddysgl	202
Trum y Gwrgedd	426
Tryfan	23
Twmpa	235
Tyrau Mawr	304
Ullscarf	174
Viewing Hill	331
Walna Scar	397
Wandope	121
Water Crag	290
Waun Fach	81
Waun Rydd	126
Waun-oer	284
Wether Hill	283
Wetherlam	132
Whernside	160

Name	Top No
Name	*Top No*
White Maiden	429
White Side	47
Whiteless Pike	308
Whiteside	205
Whiteside - East Top	183
Wild Boar Fell	204
Windy Gyle	403
Y Foel-goch	84
Y Garn (Glyders)	14
Y Garn (Moel Hebog)	365
Y Garn (Pumlumon)	248
Y Garn (Rhinogs)	375
Y Groes Fagl	311
Y Gyrn	404
Y Llethr	138
Y Lliwedd	28
Y Lliwedd - East Top	31
Yarlside	347
Yes Tor	405
Yewbarrow	378
Yockenthwaite Moor	341
Yoke	206
Yr Aran	147
Yr Elen	11
Yr Wyddfa	1
Ysgafell Wen	278
Ysgafell Wen - North Top	286
Ysgafell Wen - Far North Top	328

ANALYSIS OF THE 2000-FOOT MOUNTAIN TOPS BY GROUPS AND AREAS

Area	Group	Separate Mountains	Sub Tops	Total
Lake District	Scafell	13	30	43
	Great Gable	15	13	28
	Buttermere	9	11	20
	Skiddaw	10	8	18
	Helvellyn	13	13	26
	High Street	12	12	24
	Coniston	6	5	11
	Total	**78**	**92**	**170**
Rest of England	Cheviots	6	-	6
	Black Fell	3	1	4
	Cross Fell	15	2	17
	Burnhope Seat	10	2	12
	Great Shunner	13	7	20
	Ingleborough	14	3	17
	Peak District	2	1	3
	Dartmoor	1	1	2
	Total	**64**	**17**	**81**
North Wales	Carneddau	11	10	21
	Glyders	8	2	10
	Snowdon	7	5	12
	Moel Hebog	6	4	10
	Moelwyns	10	4	14
	Arenigs	8	4	12
	Rhinogs	6	3	9
	Arans	9	7	16
	Berwyns	9	12	21
	Cadair Idris	10	2	12
	Total	**84**	**53**	**137**

Area	Group	Separate Mountains	Sub Tops	Total
Mid & South Wales	Pumlumon	3	2	5
	Rhayader	3	-	3
	Radnor Forest	3	-	3
	Black Mountains	8	4	12
	Brecon Beacons	14	7	21
	Total	**31**	**13**	**44**
Isle of Man	Isle of Man	1	-	1
England & Wales	Wales	115	64	181
	England	142	109	251
	Total inc. IOM	**258**	**175**	**433**

BREAKDOWN OF THE 2000-FOOT MOUNTAIN TOPS BY HEIGHT BANDS

Height Band	Separate Mountains	Sub Tops	Total
1050 - 1085m	3	-	3
1000 - 1049m	1	-	1
950 - 999m	8	1	9
900 - 949m	9	4	13
850 - 899m	20	8	28
800 - 849m	24	14	38
750 - 799m	30	22	52
700 - 749m	43	32	75
650 - 699m	71	40	111
610 - 649m	54	49	103
Above 2500ft	89	43	132

Buttermere Fells and Skiddaw from High Stile (*Author*)

TABLE OF DELETED 2000-FOOT MOUNTAIN TOPS

I have included a table of deleted two-thousand foot subsidiary tops.
Most have been taken from earlier publications and have been excluded
because they do not meet the requirements of the 15 metre height
difference rule.

Group: Name	_Height_ Metres	_in_ Feet	_Grid_ Ref
Arans:			
Aran Fawddwy - North Top	850+	2788+	863228
Pen Aran (Aran Benllyn)	840+	2755+	868247
Waun Camddwr (Aran Fawddwy)	620+	2034+	848207
Arenigs:			
Carreg y Diocyn (Pen y Diocyn)	673	2207	831363
Moel Llechwedd (Arenig Fawr)	810+	2657+	829372
Berwyns:			
Bryn Gwyn (Post Gwyn)	640+	2099+	043295
Cefn Gwyntog (Cyrniau Nod)	600	1968+	975275
Moel Poethion (Moel yr Ewig)	682	2237	083307
Moel Sych - South Ridge	690+	2263+	067309
Rhos (Foel Wen)	619	2030	125323
Black Fell:			
Knoutberry Hill (Nags Head)	668	2191	803421
Nags Head (Grey Nag)	678	2224	793409
Black Mountains:			
Hay Bluff (Black Mountain)	677	2221	244366
Pen-y-garn Fawr (Black Mount'n)	616	2020	278311
Brecon Beacons:			
Duwynt (Corn Du)	824	2703	005206

Ordnance Map		Notes
1/50k	1/25k	
124/125	23	13 metres separation approx
124/125	23	9 metres separation approx
124/125	23	12 metres separation approx
124/125	18	14 metres separation approx
124/125	18	No contour ring, Less than 10 metres separation
125	846	14 metres separation
125	825	Height below 2000 feet
125	826	6 metres separation approx
125	826	12 metres separation
125	826	No contour ring, Less than 10 metres separation
86/87	31	10 metres separation approx
86/87	31	10 metres separation
161	13	11 metres separation approx
161	13	12 metres separation approx
160	11	9 metres separation

Group:	*Height*	*in*	*Grid*
Name	*Metres*	*Feet*	*Ref*

Burnhope Seat:

Black Hill (James's Hill)	645	2116	906334
Outberry Plain (James's Hill)	656	2152	938330
Stangend Rigg (Killhope Law)	634	2080	841436

Cadair Idris:

Craig Lwyd (Cadair Idris)	690	2263	714118
Mynydd Gwerngraig	680+	2230+	736136
Mynydd Pencoed	766	2513	704117

Carneddau:

Craiglwyn (Cregiau Gleision)	623	2043	731608

Cheviots:

Auchope Cairn (Cairn Hill)	720+	2362+	891198
Cairn Hill (The Cheviot)	777	2549	903195
Hangingstone Hill (Cairn Hill)	743	2437	895193

Coniston:

Brown Pike (Dow Crag)	682	2237	261966

Cross Fell:

Bullman Hills - South Top	614	2014	705371
Long Crag (Mickle Fell)	686	2250	843252
Long Fell (Little Fell)	622	2040	770198
Tinside Rigg (Little Fell)	624	2047	775199

Glyders:

Carnedd y Filiast - North Top	721	2365	618632

Ordnance Map		Notes
1/50k	1/25k	
91	31	Less than 15 metres separation
91	31	No contour ring,
		Less than 10 metre separation
86/87	31	10 metres separation
124	23	No contour ring,
		Less than 10 metres separation
124	23	9 metres separation approx
124	23	12 metres separation
115	17	14 metres separation
80	487	9 metres separation
80	487	10 metres separation
80	487	5 metres separation
96/97	6	12 metres separation approx
91	31	14 metres separation approx
91	31	7 metres height separation
91	597	14 metres separation approx
91	597	14 metres separation approx
115	17	14 metres separation approx

Group: Name	Height Metres	in Feet	Grid Ref
Great Gable: Great Scoat Fell (Little Scoat)	802	2631	154111
Middle Scoat Fell	838+	2750+	157113
Great Shunner: Swarth Fell Pike (Swarth Fell)	651	2135	761958
White Mossy Hill	659	2162	829053
Helvellyn: Calfhow Pike (Great Dodd)	660+	2166+	331211
High Crag (Helvellyn)	884	2900	343137
High Street: Adam Seat (Harter Fell)	666	2185	471091
Goat Scar (Kentmere Pike)	626	2053	473069
The Knott (High Street)	739	2424	436126
Mardale Ill Bell (High Street)	760+	2493+	448101
Ingleborough: Birks Fell	608	1994	916764
Tor Mere Top (Buckden Pike)	628	2060	970765
Radnor Forest: Great Creigiau (Black Mixen)	647	2122	198637
Scafell: Blunt Top (Scafell Pike)	901	2956	224078
Gunson Knott (Crinkle Crags)	840+	2756+	250050
Sergeant Man (High Raise)	730+	2394+	286089
Slight Side (Scafell)	762	2500	210050

| *Ordnance Map* | | *Notes* |
1/50k	*1/25k*	
89	4	No contour ring, Less than 10 metres separation
89	4	No contour ring, Less than 10 metres separation
98	617	12 metres separation
91	608	10 metres separation approx
90	5	9 metres separation
90	5	14 metres separation approx
90	5	9 metres separation
90	7	10 metres separation
90	5	13 metres separation
90	5/7	10 metres separation
98	30	Height below 2000 feet
98	30	10 metres separation approx
148	970	11 metres separation
89/90	6	One contour ring, Less than 11 metres separation
89/90	6	14 metres separation approx
89/90	6	12 metres separation approx
89/90	6	14 metres separation

Group: Name	Height Metres	in Feet	Grid Ref
Skiddaw:			
Great Sca Fell (Knott)	651	2135	291339
Knowe Crags (Blencathra)	804	2637	312271
Miller Moss (Knott)	609	1998	303334
Tarn Crags Top (Bowscale Fell)	665	2181	340310
Ullock Pike (Carl Side)	690+	2263+	244288

Ordnance Map		Notes
1/50k	*1/25k*	
89/90	576	13 metres separation
90	4	14 metres separation approx
90	576	Height below 2000 feet
90	576	14 metres separation
89/90	4	14 metres separation approx

Y Lliwedd – on the Snowdon Horseshoe (*Author*)

Chapter 2

The 500-Metre Tops of England and Wales

INTRODUCTION

As a complement to the well-established 2000 mountain list, I have
created a list of 500-metre summits. When originally compiling the list,
I used the 15 metre height difference rule, but it was soon abandoned in
favour of a 30 metre rule, this excluded many minor bumps, thereby
creating a list which is relevant and of reasonable length.
A large proportion of the 500s are on wild empty moorland hills, making
a welcome change from the more popular and overcrowded 2000-
footers. An additional seven new hill groups make their debut in the
500s, extending hill-walking possibilities in attractive areas such as the
Forest of Bowland and the Clwydian Hills. Traditional mountain sketch
maps proved unsuitable and therefore I have not included them in this
chapter. As in Chapter 1, I have included a table in altitude order with a
column for you to record your own ascents.

DEFINITION OF 500-METRE TOPS

A 500-metre top is defined as a mountain or hill exceeding 500-metres,
but below 610 metres (2000 feet) in altitude. It must be separated by
adjacent tops with a height difference of at least 30 metres on all sides.

MAP SHOWING LOCATION OF THE 500-METRE MOUNTAIN GROUPS
OF ENGLAND AND WALES

1. Scafell
2. Great Gable
3. Buttermere
4. Skiddaw
5. Helvellyn
6. High Street
7. Coniston
8. Cheviots
9. Black Fell
10. Cross Fell
11. Burnhope Seat
12. Great Shunner
13. Ingleborough
14. Forest of Bowland
15. South Pennines
16. Peak District
17. Long Mynd
18. Exmoor
19. Dartmoor
20. Carneddau
21. Clwydian Hills
22. Hiraethog
23. Snowdon
24. Moel Hebog
25. Moelwyns
26. Arenigs
27. Rhinogs
28. Arans
29. Berwyns
30. Cadair Idris
31. Pumlumon
32. Rhayader
33. Radnor Forest
34. Black Mountains
35. Brecon Beacons
36. Preseli
37. Isle of Man

TABLE OF THE 500-METRE TOPS IN GROUP ORDER

Top No	Name	Height in Metres	Feet

1. Scafell Group

Top No	Name	Metres	Feet
3	Illgill Head	609	1998
8	High Seat	608	1994
43	Bleaberry Fell	590	1935
83	Sergeant's Crag	571	1873
133	Steel Fell	553	1814
155	Hard Knott	549	1801
159	Bessyboot	548	1797
213	Calf Crag	537	1761
224	Whin Rigg	535	1755
272	Great How	522	1712

Notes   1. Summit is called Dead Pike
               2. Also named Rosthwaite Fell
               3. Also named Eskdale Fell

2. Great Gable Group

Top No	Name	Metres	Feet
30	Haystacks	597	1958
61	Middle Fell	582	1909
75	Blake Fell	573	1879
180	Carling Knott	544	1784
192	Lank Rigg	541	1774
257	Gavel Fell	526	1725
268	Crag Fell	523	1715
323	Mellbreak	512	1679
338	Hen Comb	509	1669
339	Mellbreak - North Top	509	1669

Grid Reference	Ordnance Map 1/50k	1/25k	Notes
169049	89	6	
287181	89/90	4	
286196	89/90	4	
274114	89/90	4	
319112	90	4/5	1.
232024	89/90	6	
258125	89/90	4	2.
302104	90	4/6	
152035	89	6	
198040	89/90	6	3.
193132	89/90	4	
151072	89	6	
111197	89	4	
117203	89	4	
092120	89	4	
117185	89	4	
097144	89	4	
149186	89	4	
132181	89	4	
143195	89	4	

Top No	Name	Height in Metres	Feet

3. Buttermere

63	Ard Crags	581	1906
90	Outerside	568	1863
126	Knott Rigg	556	1824
135	Lord's Seat	552	1811
259	High Snockrigg	526	1725
263	Whinlatter	525	1722

Notes   1. Also named Buttermere Moss
             2. Summit is named Whinlatter Top

4. Skiddaw

258	Great Cockup	526	1725
276	Souther Fell	522	1712
363	Dodd	502	1646

5. Helvellyn

215	Great Mell Fell	537	1761
354	Little Mell Fell	505	1656

Grid Reference	Ordnance Map 1/50k	1/25k	Notes
207198	89/90	4	
211215	89/90	4	
197189	89/90	4	
204266	89/90	4	
187169	89/90	4	1.
197249	89/90	4	2.
273333	90	576	
355292	90	5	
244274	90	4	
397254	90	5	
423240	90	5	

Top No	Name	Height in Metres	Feet

6. High Street

72	The Nab	576	1889
92	Angletarn Pikes	567	1860
134	Swinglebank Crag	553	1814
235	High Wether Howe	531	1742
240	White Howe	530	1738
247	The Forest	528	1732
265	High House Fell	524	1719
312	Sallows	516	1692
334	Beda Head	509	1669
366	High Dodd	501	1643

Notes   1. Authors name from crag on west of fell
           2. Summit is named Lord's Seat

7. Coniston

26	Black Combe	600	1968
79	Whitfell	572	1876
154	Buck Barrow	549	1801
241	Caw	529	1735

Grid Reference	Ordnance Map 1/50k	1/25k	Notes
434152	90	5	
413148	90	5	
501049	90	7	1.
515109	90	5	
524042	90	7	
528036	90	7	
518067	90	7	2.
437040	90	7	
428171	90	5	
415182	90	5	
136855	96	625	
159930	96	6	
152910	96	6	
231945	96	6	

Top No	Name	Height in Metres	Feet

8. The Cheviot Hills

Top No	Name	Metres	Feet
23	Peel Fell	602	1975
25 ✓	The Schil	601	1971
66	Carter Fell - North Top	579	1899
82	Deadwater Fell	571	1873
86	Dunmoor Hill	569	1866
104	Wether Cairn	563	1847
106 ✓	Beefstand Hill	562	1843
118	Thirl Moor	558	1830
136	Wool Meath	552	1811
153	Black Hag	549	1801
186	Yarnspath Law	543	1781
216	Newton Tors	537	1761
250	Shill Moor	528	1732
254	Ravens Knowe	527	1728
260	Preston Hill	526	1725
300	Sighty Crag	518	1699
301	Broadhope Hill	517	1696
316	Glendhu Hill	514	1686
321	Monkside	513	1683
333	Lint Lands	510	1673
343	Brownhart Law	508	1666
367	Hungry Law	501	1643
368	Shillhope Law	501	1643

Notes   1. Second top of the same height 110 metres to the west
2. Summit on English Scottish border
3. Summit on English Scottish border
4. Also named Wholhope Hill
5. Summit on English Scottish border
6. DANGER AREA - military range
7. Also named Oh Me Edge

Grid Reference	Ordnance Map 1/50k	1/25k	Notes
626997	80	509	1.
869223	74	475	2
682052	80	498	3.
626972	80	509	
967182	81	487	
941116	80	487	4.
821144	80	487	5
806084	80	499	6.
702998	80	509	7.
861237	74	475	8.
884132	80	487	
908269	74/75	475	
944153	80	487	
780062	80	498	9.
923238	74/75	475	
601809	80	521	
933234	74/75	475	
568864	80	520	10.
685950	80	509	11.
903163	80	487	
788094	80	498	12.
747061	80	498	13.
873097	80	499	

8. Also named Corbie Craig
9. Summit is named Ravens Pike
10. Summit on English Scottish border
11. Also named Hogswood Moor
12. Roman signal station
13. Summit on English Scottish border

Top No	Name	Height in Metres	Feet

9. Black Fell

Top No	Name	Metres	Feet
6	Thack Moor	609	1998
40	Blotting Raise	591	1938
330	Park Fell	511	1676

Notes   1. Also named Croglin Fell
          2. Also see Pathfinder Map No 569

10. Cross Fell

Top No	Name	Metres	Feet
35	Murton Pike	594	1948
36	Roman Fell	594	1948
103	Iron Band	563	1847
198	Cuns Fell	539	1768
290	Brownber Hill	519	1702
309	Great Knipe	516	1692

Notes   1. Also spot height of 516m 200 metres west

Grid Reference	Ordnance Map 1/50k	1/25k	Notes
611463	86	569	
597495	86	568	1.
697455	86	31	2.
735231	91	31	
754203	91	31	
837188	91/92	598	
648368	91	578	
706275	91	31	
867145	91/92	598	1.

Top No	Name	Height in Metres	Feet

11. Burnhope Seat

Top No	Name	Metres	Feet
64	Alston Moor	580+	1902+
95	Dry Rigg	566	1856
170	Hard Rigg	546	1791
195	Bolt's Law	540	1771
262	Pike Rigg	525	1722
264	Ayle Common	524	1719
295	Horseshoe Hill	519	1702
308	Collier Law	516	1692

Notes   1. Also named Middle Fell
         2. Also named Redburn Common

12. Great Shunner

Top No	Name	Metres	Feet
11	Arant Haw	605	1984
13	Green Bell	605	1984
51	Simon's Seat	587	1925
54	Hooksey	586	1922
59	Great Pinseat	583	1912
67	Hazelgill Knott	578	1896
74	Kensgriff	574	1883
100	Pickerstone Ridge	565	1853
131	Hoove	553	1814
142	Tarn Seat	551	1807
165	Nateby Common	547	1794
190	West Fell	542	1778
233	Uldale Head	532	1745
274	High Greygrits	522	1712
278	Harter Fell	521	1709
287	Moudy Mea	520+	1706+

Notes   1. Also named Tarn Rigg

Grid Reference	Ordnance Map 1/50k	1/25k	Notes
750437	86/87	31	1.
907448	87	570	2.
750488	86/87	569	
950454	87	570	
730539	86/87	559	3.
724510	86/87	559	4.
985449	87	570	
016418	87	571	

3. Also named Whitfield Moor
4. Summit is named Tarn Rigg

662946	98	617	
699011	91	607	
660000	91/97/98	617	
685009	91	607	
970027	91/92	30	
673997	98	617	
688993	98	617	
995946	98	30	
005073	92	30	
956943	98	30	1.
803054	91/92	608	2.
670015	91	607	
641000	91	607	
877089	91/92	30	
721002	91	607	
871117	91/92	598	

2. Also named Tailbridge Hill

Top No	Name	Height in Metres	Feet

13. Ingleborough

Top No	Name	Metres	Feet
1	Calf Top	609	1998
2	Horse Head Moor	609	1998
15	Little Whernside	604	1981
21	Cosh Knott	602	1975
57	Brown Haw	584	1915
73	Meugher	575	1886
77	Naughtberry Hill	573	1879
119	Wold Fell	558	1830
123	Aye Gill Pike	556	1824
129	Grizdales	553	1814
130	Height of Hazely	553	1814
166	Rye Loaf Hill	547	1794
168	Dead Man's Hill	546	1791
176	Redshaw Moss	545	1788
204	Castle Knott	538	1765
211	Parson's Pulpit	538	1765
220	Blea Moor	535	1755
221	Harland Hill	535	1755
236	Proctor High Mark	531	1742
350	Burnsall and Thorpe Fell	506	1660
360	Cam Rakes	503	1650

Notes
1. Summit is named Sugar Loaf
2. Also named Upper Stone Haw
3. Also named Snaizeholme Fell
4. Also named Carlton Moor

Grid Reference	Ordnance Map		Notes
	1/50k	1/25k	
664856	98	2	
894768	98	30	1.
028776	98	30	
845784	98	2/30	
995799	98	30	
044704	98	10	
977818	98	30	
791851	98	2	
721886	98	2	
868643	98	10	
037860	98	30	
864633	98	10	2.
058783	98	30	
813846	98	2	3.
656842	97	628	
918688	98	10	
773826	98	2	
028843	98	30	4.
937677	98	10	
009597	104	10	
840810	98	2/30	

Top No	Name	Height in Metres	Feet

14. Forest of Bowland

Top No	Name	Metres	Feet
111	Ward's Stone	561	1840
184	White Hill	544	1784
255	Wolfhole Crag	527	1728
285	Fair Snape Fell	520+	1706+

15. South Pennines

Top No	Name	Metres	Feet
121	Pendle Hill	557	1827
303	Lad Law	517	1696

Notes   1. Summit is named Beacon or Big End
           2. Also named Boulsworth Hill

Grid Reference	Ordnance Map 1/50k	1/25k	Notes
593587	102	659	
674588	103	660	
634578	102/103	660	
597473	102	668	
804414	103	670	1.
930355	103	21	2.

Top No	Name	Height in Metres	Feet

16. Peak District

Top No	Name	Metres	Feet
60	Black Hill	582	1909
85	Brown Knoll	569	1866
114	Shining Tor	559	1833
138	Axe Edge Moor	551	1807
149	Howden Edge	550	1804
152	Axe Edge	549	1801
173	Whetstone Ridge	545+	1788+
182	Featherbed Top	544	1784
183	Mill Hill	544	1784
187	Black Chew Head	542	1778
193	Lord's Seat	540+	1771+
202	Back Tor	538	1765
284	Cats Tor	520+	1706+
304	Mam Tor	517	1696
322	Oliver Hill	513	1683
346	Black Edge	507	1663
351	Shutlingsloe	506	1660
356	The Roaches	505	1656
373	West Nab	500	1640

Notes   1. West Yorkshire county top. Summit is named Soldier's Lump
             2. Cheshire county top
             3. South Yorkshire county top. Summit is named High Stones
             4. Also named Featherbed Moss
             5. Same height as Featherbed Top 3km to north west
             6. Greater Manchester Co Top 15m south west of spot height
             7. Also named Rushup Edge
             8. Also named Withinleach Moor

Grid Reference	Ordnance Map 1/50k	1/25k	Notes
078047	110	1	1.
084851	110	1	
995737	118	24	2.
035706	119	24	
188944	110	1	3.
032693	119	24	
002709	119	24	
091921	110	1	4.
061904	110	1	5.
056020	110	1	6.
110834	110	1	7.
198910	110	1	
995759	118	24	8.
128836	110	1	
027676	119	24	
062770	119	24	
977696	118	24	
001639	119	24	
077088	110	714	

Top No	Name	Height in Metres	Feet

17. Long Mynd

Top No	Name	Metres	Feet
196 ✓	Brown Clee Hill	540	1771
219	Stiperstones	536	1758
228 ✓	Titterstone Clee Hill	533	1748
310 ✓	The Long Mynd	516	1692
320	Corndon Hill	513	1683
332 ✓	Clee Burf	510	1673

Notes
1. Summit is named Abdon Burf. Shropshire county top
2. Summit is named Manstone Rock
3. Summit is named Giant's Chair
4. Summit is named Pole Bank

18. Exmoor

Top No	Name	Metres	Feet
293	Dunkery Beacon	519	1702

Notes
1. Somerset county top. Also named Dunkery Hill

Grid Reference	Ordnance Map 1/50k	1/25k	Notes
594867	137/138	931	1.
368986	137	909	2.
591779	137/138	951	3.
415944	137	910	4.
306969	137	909	
594843	137/138	931	
891416	181	9	1.

Top No	Name	Height in Metres	Feet

19. Dartmoor

Top No	Name	Metres	Feet
18	Cut Hill	603	1978
20	Hangingstone Hill	603	1978
53	Great Links Tor	586	1922
56	Amicombe Hill	584	1915
147	Cosdon Hill	550	1804
208	Great Mis Tor	538	1765
230	Hamel Down	532	1745
252	Higher White Tor	527	1728
307	North Hessary Tor	517	1696
315	Ryder's Hill	515	1689
352	White Ridge	506	1660

Notes   1. Summit is named Cosdon Beacon
         2. Summit is named Broad Barrow

20. Carneddau

Top No	Name	Metres	Feet
19	Foel Lwyd	603	1978
65	Moel Wnion	580	1902
115	Yr Orsedd	559	1833
160	Craig Wen	548	1797
171	Moel Eilio	546	1791
189	Gyrn	542	1778
218	Foel-ganol	536	1758

Grid Reference	Ordnance Map 1/50k	1/25k	Notes
598827	191	28	
617861	191	28	
551868	191	28	
568872	191	28	
636915	191	28	1.
563769	191	28	
706799	191	28	2.
620786	191	28	
579742	191	28	
660691	202	28	
648821	191	28	
720723	115	17	
650697	115	17	
694715	115	17	
729603	115	17	
747659	115	17	
647688	115	17	
688716	115	17	

Top No	Name	Height in Metres	Feet

21. Clwydian Hills

Top No	Name	Metres	Feet
71	Moel y Gamelin	577	1893
96	Cyrn-y-Brain	565	1853
128	Moel Fammau	554	1817
157	Moel Morfydd	549	1801
161	Moel y Faen	548	1797
326	Eglwyseg Mountain	511	1676
327	Foel Fenlli	511	1676
357	Moel y Gaer	504	1653

Notes
1. Also named Maesyrychen Mountain
2. Site of Jubilee Tower
3. Also named Llantysilio Mountain
4. Also named Ruabon Mountain
5. Site of hill fort

22. Hiraethog

Top No	Name	Metres	Feet
231	Mwdwl-eithin	532	1745
294	Foel Gôch	519	1702
298	Gorsedd Brân	518	1699
362	Craig Bron-banog	502	1646

Note
1. Also named Marial Gwyn
2. Second top of same height 200m WNW

23. Snowdon

Top No	Name	Metres	Feet
13	Foel Goch	605	1984

Grid Reference	Ordnance Map 1/50k	1/25k	Notes
177465	116	805	1.
208489	117	806	
162626	116	772	2.
160458	116	805	3.
185475	116	805	
231463	117	806	4.
165601	116	772	
167464	116	805	5.
917541	116	787	
000556	116	787	1.
969597	116	787	
019520	116	788	2.
571564	115	17	

Top No	Name	Height in Metres	Feet

24. Moel Hebog

Top No	Name	Metres	Feet
4	Mynydd Graig Goch	609	1998
102	Yr Eifl	564	1850
132	Moel-ddu	553	1814
273	Gyrn Ddu	522	1712
291	Bryn Banog	519	1702
335	Bwlch Mawr	509	1669

Notes   1. Summit is named Graig Goch
             2. Also named Ffridd Uchaf

25. Moelwyns

Top No	Name	Metres	Feet
9	Moel Meirch	607	1991
38	Y Ro Wen	594	1948
41	Carnedd y Cribau	591	1938
47	Yr Arddu	589	1932
49	Y Gamallt	588	1929
69	Moel Farlwyd	577	1893
137	Y Garnedd	552	1811
253	Pen y Bedw	527	1728
266	Moel Dyrnogydd	524	1719
329	Manod Bach	511	1676
364	Moel Gamallt	502	1646

Notes   1. Also named Graig Goch
             2. Authors name from Llynnau Gamallt 300 metres west

Grid Reference	Ordnance Map 1/50k	1/25k	Notes
497486	115/123	17	1.
365447	123	801	
580442	124	18	
401468	115/123	801	
576456	115	17	2.
427478	115/123	801	
661504	115	17	
745498	115	18	
676537	115	17	
673507	115	17	
752447	124	18	1.
707487	115	18	
742431	124	18	
779470	115	18	
695491	115	18	
714447	124	18	
744441	124	18	2.

Top No	Name	Height in Metres	Feet

26. Arenigs

Top No	Name	Metres	Feet
33	Foel-boeth	596	1955
70	Moel y Feidiog	577	1893
87	Garnedd Fawr	569	1866
125	Graig Wen	556	1824
150	Moel Ymenyn	550	1804
156	Moel Emoel	549	1801
194	Mynydd Bryn-llech	540+	1771+
203	Carnedd Lago	538	1765
214	Graig Ddu	537	1761
227	Garn Prŷs	533	1748
238	Mynydd Nodal	530+	1738+
246	Foel Fawr	528	1732
269	Craig yr Hafod	523	1715
280	Moel y Gydros	521	1709
283	Bryn-pig	520+	1706+
286	Moel Cae'r-defaid	520+	1706+
289	Rhobell Ganol	520+	1706+
292	Craig Dolfudr - North Top	519	1702
297	Craig Dolfudr	518	1699
325	Bryn-mawr	511	1676
358	Rhobell-y-big	504	1653
361	Moel Oernant	503	1650
372	Ffridd yr Allt-llŵyd	500	1640

Notes
1. Also named Cyfiau
2. Also named Moel Llechwedd-figyn
3. Second top of similar height 450 metres ESE entitled Craig y Benglog

Grid Reference	Ordnance Map 1/50k	1/25k	Notes
865431	124/125	18	
781324	124	18	
938423	125	18	
739395	124	18	
840346	124/125	18	
938402	125	18	
805314	124/125	18	
783406	124	18	
888429	124/125	18	
887484	116	18	
865393	124/125	18	
726395	124	18	
889437	124/125	18	1.
914454	116	18	2.
767306	124	18	
801246	124	23	3.
786275	124	23	
822317	124/125	18	
828310	124/125	18	
801443	124/125	18	
783283	124	23	
742340	124	18	
797296	124	18	

Top No	Name	Height in Metres	Feet

27. Rhinogs

32	Craig Ddrwg	596	1955
45	Craig y Grut	589	1932
46	Moelfre	589	1932
93	Craig Wion	566	1856
299	Moel Morwynion	518	1699
305	Mynydd Egryn	517	1696

Notes   1. Authors name from llyn 600 metres to south west

28. Arans

10	Moel y Pawl	606	1988
24	Y Gribin	602	1975
29	Moel Llygoed	598	1961
44	Foel Figenau	590	1935
88	Mynydd Coch	569	1866
89	Moel Eunant	568	1863
116	Bryn Glâs	558	1830
177	Tir Rhiwiog	545	1788
185	Foel Benddin	543	1781
201	Rhiwaedog-uwch-afon	539	1768
232	Mynydd Maes-glas	532	1745
267	Carnedd Wen	523	1715
318	Pen Foel-y-ffridd	514	1686

Notes   1. Name from bwlch to the NE
             2. Name from cwm to the west
             3. Also Mynydd Clywedog

Grid Reference	Ordnance Map 1/50k	1/25k	Notes
657332	124	18	
631211	124	18	
626246	124	18	
664320	124	18	
664306	124	18	1.
623195	124	18	
919257	125	23	1.
843177	124/125	23	
925194	125	23	2.
917284	125	23	
939197	125	23	
947239	125	23	
923215	125	23	
929161	125	23	
854165	124/125	23	
939313	125	18	
915147	125	23	3.
924099	125	23	
892188	124/125	23	

Top No	Name	Height in Metres	Feet

29. Berwyns

Top No	Name	Metres	Feet
7	Glan-hafon	608	1994
39	Cerrig Coediog	593	1945
48	Rhwng y Ddwynant	588	1929
58	Moel yr Henfaes	584	1915
105	Y Fawnen	563	1847
145	Vivod Mountain	550+	1804+
197	Rhialgwm	540	1771
200	Ffordd Gefn	539	1768
225	Mynydd Mawr	534	1751
270	Gyrn Moelfre	523	1715
277	Carnedd Dâs Eithin	521	1709
279	Moel Hen-fache	521	1709
302	Cyrniau y Llyn	517	1696

Notes   1. Name from marsh 600 metres west
         2. Also named Bryn Gwyn
         3. Also named Dâs Eithin
         4. Also see Pathfinder map 846

Grid Reference	Ordnance Map 1/50k	1/25k	Notes
078274	125	846	
113386	125	826	
978248	125	23	
077386	125	826	
145360	125	826	1.
170400	125	826	
055212	125	846	
034241	125	846	2.
133286	125	846	
184294	125	846	
051239	125	846	3.
110282	125	846	
000245	125	23	4.

Top No	Name	Height in Metres	Feet

30. Cadair Idris

Top No	Name	Metres	Feet
12	Craig Portas	605	1984
31	Mynydd Braich-gôch	597	1958
50	Craig Portas - East Top	587	1925
52	Graig Goch	586	1922
144	Tarren Cwm-ffernol	550+	1804+
167	Braich Ddu	546	1791
174	Ceiswyn	545	1788
317	Mynydd Fron-fraith	514	1686
324	Pen Trum-gwr	512	1679
344	Godre Fynydd	508	1666
370	Esgair Berfa	500+	1640+

Notes 1. Also named Craig Cwm-llwyd
       2. Summit is named Mwdl Eithin

Grid Reference	Ordnance Map 1/50k	1/25k	Notes
802141	124	23	
729073	124	23	
808143	124	23	
715085	124	23	
659024	135	23	
645121	124	23	1.
745109	124	23	2.
748117	124	23	
651030	135	23	
757097	124	23	
637096	124	23	

Top No	Name	Height in Metres	Feet

31. Pumlumon

Top No	Name	Metres	Feet
62	Siambr Trawsfynydd	582	1909
94	Drybedd	566	1856
97	Foel Uchaf	565	1853
101	Foel Fadian	564	1850
112	Banc Llechwedd-mawr	560	1837
139	Banc Bugeilyn	551	1807
148	Drosgol	550	1804
172	Y Foel	546	1791
179	Bryn y Fedwen	544	1784
209	Llechwedd Hirgoed -West Top	538	1765
222	Llechwedd Hirgoed	535	1755
242	Foel Fras	529	1735
243	Foel Grafiau	529	1735
244	Moel Hyddgen	529	1735
281	Moel y Llyn	521	1709
282	Banc Bwlchygarreg	520+	1706+
347	Disgwylfa Fawr	507	1663
348	Pen Creigiau'r Llan	507	1663
369	Banc yr Wyn	500+	1640+

Notes   1. Also see Pathfinder map 907
        2. Same height as Foel Fras 600 metres to the north
        3. Authors name from bwlch 600 metres to the south
        4. Also named Fainc Fawr

Grid Reference	Ordnance Map 1/50k	1/25k	Notes
800932	135	885	1.
772834	135	927	
803912	135/136	907	
828954	135/136	907	
775898	135	927	
827924	135/136	907	
760879	135	927	
839842	135/136	928	
841953	135/136	907	
814837	135/136	928	
821832	135/136	928	
766926	135	23	
765920	135	23	2.
764943	135	23	3.
713917	135	23	
730918	135	23	
737847	135	927	
745939	135	23	
742902	135	23	4.

Top No	Name	Height in Metres	Feet

32. Rhayader

Top No	Name	Metres	Feet
16	Y Gamriw	604	1981
37	Waun Claerddu	594	1948
55	Pegwn Mawr	586	1922
76	Cefn Croes	573	1879
78	Geifas	572	1876.
81	Crugyn Llwyd	571	1873
84	Draws Drum	570+	1870+
108	Bryn Du	562	1843
113	Llechwedd Ddu	559	1833
158	Pant-llwyd	549	1801
162	Mynydd Tywi	548	1797
164	Blaen Rhestr	547	1794
175	Mynydd Tywi - East Top	545	1788
191	Garn Gron	541	1774
199	Craig Dyfnant	539	1768
205	Cerrig Gwaun-y-llan	538	1765
206	Drum Ddu	538	1765
207	Esgair y Llwyn	538	1765

Notes

1. Summit named Carnyrhyrddod
2. Also see Pathfinder Map No 928
3. Also named Ffos Bryn-du
4. Summit named Carnbwlchcloddiau
5. Also top of same height at grid ref 832692, see Pathfinder map 969
6. Authors name from Tywi Forest
7. Summit named Carn-y-geifr

Grid Reference	Ordnance Map 1/50k	1/25k	Notes
944612	147	969	
791704	135/147	947	1.
024812	136	929	
808800	135/136/147	948	2.
819728	135/136/147	948	
024796	136/147	949	
791810	135	927	
846801	135/136	928	3.
854787	135/136/147	948	4.
835706	135/136/147	948	5.
774606	146/147	968	6.
844694	135/136/147	969	
779606	146/147	968	
740611	146/147	968	
875656	135/136/147	969	
866780	135/136/147	948	
971604	147	969	7.
894735	135/136/147	948	

Top No	Name	Height in Metres	Feet

32. Rhayader (continued)

Top No	Name	Metres	Feet
212	Banc Dolwen	537	1761
226	Esgair Penygarreg	533	1748
239	Dibyn Du	530	1738
251	Cefn y Cnwc	527	1728
256	Esgair Ganol	526	1725
261	Crug Gynon	525	1722
275	Moelfryn	522	1712
288	Pen Lan-fawr	520+	1706+
306	Mynydd Trawsnant	517	1696
328	Garn Wen	511	1676
331	Penrhiw-wen	510+	1673+
336	Camlo Hill	509	1669
337	Gopa Uchaf	509	1669
342	Brondre-fawr Hill	508	1666
345	Sychnentydd	508	1666
353	Coed Nant-yr-hwch	505	1656
355	Moel Hywel	505	1656

Notes   8. Summit named Crugyn Ci
            9. Source of River Tywi 700M south
          10. Also named Llethr Garw

Grid Reference	Ordnance Map 1/50k	1/25k	Notes
793787	135/147	947	
927688	136/147	969	8.
791655	135/147	968	
773589	146/147	990	
879772	135/136/147	948	
802638	147	969	9.
935721	136/147	948	
890749	135/136/147	948	10.
821484	147	1014	
845460	147	1014	
925709	136/147	948	
037698	136/147	970	
729590	146/147	990	
042783	136/147	949	
910725	136/147	948	
818554	147	991	
003713	136/147	949	

Top No	Name	Height in Metres	Feet

33. Radnor Forest

Top No	Name	Metres	Feet
28	Whimble	599	1965
163	Beacon Hill	547	1794
169	Fron-wen	546	1791
188	Gwaunceste Hill	542	1778
210	Nyth-grug	538	1765
229	Colva Hill	532	1745
245	Cilfaesty Hill	528	1732
248	Gors Lydan	528	1732
271	Glascwm Hill	522	1712
296	Bryn Coch	518	1699
311	Pool Hill	516	1692
340	Red Hill	509	1669
349	Warren Hill	507	1663

Notes   1. Also named Llanfihangel Hill

34. Black Mountains

Top No	Name	Metres	Feet
5	Mynydd Troed	609	1998
34	Y-fâl or Sugar Loaf	596	1955
234	Hatterrall Hill	531	1742
314	Mynydd Llangorse	515	1689

Grid Reference	Ordnance Map		Notes
	1/50k	*1/25k*	
205626	137/148	971	
177768	136/148	949	
181660	136/148	970	
158555	148	992	
171607	148	970	
195554	148	992	1.
128841	136	929	
126769	136/148	949	
170525	148	992	
125849	136	929	
177754	136/148	949	
156501	148	992	
144778	136/148	949	
166292	161	13	
273188	161	13	
308257	161	13	
159267	161	13	

Top No	Name	Height in Metres	Feet

35. Brecon Beacons

Top No	Name	Metres	Feet
17	Yr Allt	604	1981
22	Foel Fraith	602	1975
27	Cefnffordd	600	1968
42	Moel Feity	591	1938
68	Mynydd Coety	578	1896
80	Cefn Coch	571	1873
91	Werfa	568	1863
99	Pant y Creigiau	565	1853
107	Bryn	562	1843
109	Waun Leuci	562	1843
110	Blorenge	561	1840
117	Carreg Goch	558	1830
120	Mynydd Llanynidr	557	1827
122	Twyn Crugyrafan	556+	1824+
124	Cefn y Cylchau	556	1824
127	Mynydd Caerau	555	1820
141	Gwastad	551	1807
143	Tor y Foel	551	1807
151	Mynydd Carn-y-cefn	550	1804
181	Disgwylfa	544	1784
223	Mynydd Ton	535	1755
237	Carn Pen-rhiw-ddu	530+	1738+
249	Mynydd Blaengwynfi	528	1732
313	Hirwaun Common	515	1689
319	Allt Forgan	513	1683
341	Twynwalter	509	1670
359	Y Domen Fawr	504	1653
365	Mynydd Ynyscorrwg	502	1646

Notes   1. West Glamorgan county top, also named Craig y Llyn
         2. Summit named Twyn Ffynhonnau Goerion
         3. Also named Pen y Bryn
         4. Also named Cefn Cul
         5. Also named Blorens
         6. Summit is named Garn Fawr

Grid Reference	Ordnance Map 1/50k	1/25k	Notes
905201	160	11	
757183	160	12	
907031	170	1108	1.
849230	160	12	
232080	161	1110	2.
221093	161	1110	
913948	170	1128	
057162	160	11	
071227	160	11	3.
862206	160	12	4.
270119	161	1086	5.
819170	160	12	
124151	161	11	6.
921955	170	1128	7.
757197	160	12	
890945	170	1128	8.
235055	161	1110	
115195	161	11	
187085	161	1109	
816179	160	12	9.
949941	170	1128	
726187	160	12	10.
906974	170	1128	
943035	170	1108	11.
066178	160	11	
828175	160	12	
166072	161	1109	
887980	170	1128	

7. Summit is named Crug yr Afan
8. Summit is named Llyndwr Fawr
9. Summit is named Sinc Giedd
10. Also named Pen Rhiw-ddu
11. Also named Craig-y-bwlch

Top No	Name	Height in Metres	Feet

36. Preseli

| 217 | Foel Cwmcerwyn | 536 | 1758 |

37. Isle of Man

98	North Barrule	565	1853
140	Clagh Ouyr	551	1807
146	Clagh Ouyr - North Top	550	1804
178	Beinn-y-phott	544	1784
371	Carraghan	500	1640

Grid Reference	Ordnance Map 1/50k	1/25k	Notes
094312	145	1033	
443909	95		
414889	95		
426900	95		
381860	95		
369849	95		

TABLE OF THE 500-METRE TOPS IN ORDER OF ALTITUDE

Top No	Name	Group
1	Calf Top	Ingleborough
2	Horse Head Moor	Ingleborough
3	Illgill Head	Scafell
4	Mynydd Graig Goch	Moel Hebog
5	Mynydd Troed	Black Mountains
6	Thack Moor	Black Fell
7	Glan-hafon	Berwyns
8	High Seat	Scafell
9	Moel Meirch	Moelwyns
10	Moel y Pawl	Arans
11	Arant Haw	Great Shunner
12	Craig Portas	Cadair Idris
13	Foel Goch	Snowdon
14	Green Bell	Great Shunner
15	Little Whernside	Ingleborough
16	Y Gamriw	Rhayader
17	Yr Allt	Brecon Beacons
18	Cut Hill	Dartmoor
19	Foel Lwyd	Carneddau
20	Hangingstone Hill	Dartmoor
21	Cosh Knott	Ingleborough
22	Foel Fraith	Brecon Beacons
23	Peel Fell	Cheviots
24	Y Gribin	Arans
25	The Schil	Cheviots
26	Black Combe	Coniston
27	Cefnffordd	Brecon Beacons
28	Whimble	Radnor Forest
29	Moel Llygoed	Arans
30	Haystacks	Great Gable
31	Mynydd Braich-gôch	Cadair Idris

Height in Metres	Date Ascended/Notes
609	_____
609	_____
609	_____
609	_____
609	_____
609	_____
608	_____
608	_____
607	_____
606	_____
605	_____
605	_____
605	_____
605	_____
604	_____
604	_____
604	_____
603	_____
603	_____
603	_____
602	_____
602	_____
602	_____
602	_____
601	_____
600	_____
600	_____
599	_____
598	_____
597	_____
597	_____

Top No	Name	Group
32	Craig Ddrwg	Rhinogs
33	Foel-boeth	Arenigs
34	Y-fâl or Sugar Loaf	Black Mountains
35	Murton Pike	Cross Fell
36	Roman Fell	Cross Fell
37	Waun Claerddu	Rhayader
38	Y Ro Wen	Moelwyns
39	Cerrig Coediog	Berwyns
40	Blotting Raise	Black Fell
41	Carnedd y Cribau	Moelwyns
42	Moel Feity	Brecon Beacons
43	Bleaberry Fell	Scafell
44	Foel Figenau	Arans
45	Craig y Grut	Rhinogs
46	Moelfre	Rhinogs
47	Yr Arddu	Moelwyns
48	Rhwng y Ddwynant	Berwyns
49	Y Gamallt	Moelwyns
50	Craig Portas - East Top	Cadair Idris
51	Simon's Seat	Great Shunner
52	Graig Goch	Cadair Idris
53	Great Links Tor	Dartmoor
54	Hooksey	Great Shunner
55	Pegwn Mawr	Rhayader
56	Amicombe Hill	Dartmoor
57	Brown Haw	Ingleborough
58	Moel yr Henfaes	Berwyns
59	Great Pinseat	Great Shunner
60	Black Hill	Peak District
61	Middle Fell	Great Gable
62	Siambr Trawsfynydd	Pumlumon
63	Ard Crags	Buttermere
64	Alston Moor	Burnhope Seat

Height in Metres	*Date Ascended/Notes*
596	
596	
596	
594	
594	
594	
594	
593	
591	
591	
591	
590	
590	
589	
589	
589	
588	
588	
587	
587	
586	
586	
586	
586	
584	
584	
584	
583	
582	
582	
582	
581	
580+	

Top No	Name	Group
65	Moel Wnion	Carneddau
66	Carter Fell - North	Cheviots
67	Hazelgill Knott	Great Shunner
68	Mynydd Coety	Brecon Beacons
69	Moel Farlwyd	Moelwyns
70	Moel y Feidiog	Arenigs
71	Moel y Gamelin	Clwydian Hills
72	The Nab	High Street
73	Meugher	Ingleborough
74	Kensgriff	Great Shunner
75	Blake Fell	Great Gable
76	Cefn Croes	Rhayader
77	Naughtberry Hill	Ingleborough
78	Geifas	Rhayader
79	Whitfell	Coniston
80	Cefn Coch	Brecon Beacons
81	Crugyn Llwyd	Rhayader
82	Deadwater Fell	Cheviots
83	Sergeant's Crag	Scafell
84	Draws Drum	Rhayader
85	Brown Knoll	Peak District
86	Dunmoor Hill	Cheviots
87	Garnedd Fawr	Arenigs
88	Mynydd Coch	Arans
89	Moel Eunant	Arans
90	Outerside	Buttermere
91	Werfa	Brecon Beacons
92	Angletarn Pikes	High Street
93	Craig Wion	Rhinogs
94	Drybedd	Pumlumon
95	Dry Rigg	Burnhope Seat
96	Cyrn-y-Brain	Clwydian Hills
97	Foel Uchaf	Pumlumon

Height in Metres	Date Ascended/Notes
580	
579	_____
578	_____
578	_____
577	_____
577	_____
577	_____
576	_____
575	_____
574	_____
573	_____
573	_____
573	_____
572	_____
572	_____
571	_____
571	_____
571	_____
571	_____
570+	_____
569	_____
569	_____
569	_____
569	_____
568	_____
568	_____
568	_____
567	_____
566	_____
566	_____
566	_____
565	_____
565	_____

Top No	Name	Group
98	North Barrule	Isle of Man
99	Pant y Creigiau	Brecon Beacons
100	Pickerstone Ridge	Great Shunner
101	Foel Fadian	Pumlumon
102	Yr Eifl	Moel Hebog
103	Iron Band	Cross Fell
104	Wether Cairn	Cheviots
105	Y Fawnen	Berwyns
106	Beefstand Hill	Cheviots
107	Bryn	Brecon Beacons
108	Bryn Du	Rhayader
109	Waun Leuci	Brecon Beacons
110	Blorenge	Brecon Beacons
111	Ward's Stone	Bowland Forest
112	Banc Llechwedd-mawr	Pumlumon
113	Llechwedd Ddu	Rhayader
114	Shining Tor	Peak District
115	Yr Orsedd	Carneddau
116	Bryn Glâs	Arans
117	Carreg Goch	Brecon Beacons
118	Thirl Moor	Cheviots
119	Wold Fell	Ingleborough
120	Mynydd Llanynidr	Brecon Beacons
121	Pendle Hill	South Pennines
122	Twyn Crugyrafan	Brecon Beacons
123	Aye Gill Pike	Ingleborough
124	Cefn y Cylchau	Brecon Beacons
125	Graig Wen	Arenigs
126	Knott Rigg	Buttermere
127	Mynydd Caerau	Brecon Beacons
128	Moel Fammau	Clwydian Hills
129	Grizdales	Ingleborough
130	Height of Hazely	Ingleborough

Height in Metres	Date Ascended/Notes
565	_____
565	_____
565	_____
564	_____
564	_____
563	_____
563	_____
563	_____
562	_____
562	_____
562	_____
562	_____
561	_____
561	_____
560	_____
559	_____
559	_____
559	_____
558	_____
558	_____
558	_____
558	_____
557	_____
557	_____
556+	_____
556	_____
556	_____
556	_____
556	_____
555	_____
554	_____
553	_____
553	_____

Top No	Name	Group
131	Hoove	Great Shunner
132	Moel-ddu	Moel Hebog
133	Steel Fell	Scafell
134	Swinglebank Crag	High Street
135	Lord's Seat	Buttermere
136	Wool Meath	Cheviots
137	Y Garnedd	Moelwyns
138	Axe Edge Moor	Peak District
139	Banc Bugeilyn	Pumlumon
140	Clagh Ouyr	Isle of Man
141	Gwastad	Brecon Beacons
142	Tarn Seat	Great Shunner
143	Tor y Foel	Brecon Beacons
144	Tarren Cwm-ffernol	Cadair Idris
145	Vivod Mountain	Berwyns
146	Clagh Ouyr - North Top	Isle of Man
147	Cosdon Hill	Dartmoor
148	Drosgol	Pumlumon
149	Howden Edge	Peak District
150	Moel Ymenyn	Arenigs
151	Mynydd Carn-y-cefn	Brecon Beacons
152	Axe Edge	Peak District
153	Black Hag	Cheviots
154	Buck Barrow	Coniston
155	Hard Knott	Scafell
156	Moel Emoel	Arenigs
157	Moel Morfydd	Clwydian Hills
158	Pant-llwyd	Rhayader
159	Bessyboot	Scafell
160	Craig Wen	Carneddau
161	Moel y Faen	Clwydian Hills
162	Mynydd Tywi	Rhayader
163	Beacon Hill	Radnor Forest

Height in Metres	*Date Ascended/Notes*
553	_____
553	_____
553	_____
553	_____
552	_____
552	_____
552	_____
551	_____
551	_____
551	_____
551	_____
551	_____
551	_____
550+	_____
550+	_____
550	_____
550	_____
550	_____
550	_____
550	_____
550	_____
549	_____
549	_____
549	_____
549	_____
549	_____
549	_____
549	_____
548	_____
548	_____
548	_____
548	_____
547	_____

Top No	Name	Group
164	Blaen Rhestr	Rhayader
165	Nateby Common	Great Shunner
166	Rye Loaf Hill	Ingleborough
167	Braich Ddu	Cadair Idris
168	Dead Man's Hill	Ingleborough
169	Fron-wen	Radnor Forest
170	Hard Rigg	Burnhope Seat
171	Moel Eilio	Carneddau
172	Y Foel	Pumlumon
173	Whetstone Ridge	Peak District
174	Ceiswyn	Cadair Idris
175	Mynydd Tywi - East Top	Rhayader
176	Redshaw Moss	Ingleborough
177	Tir Riwiog	Arans
178	Beinn-y-phott	Isle of Man
179	Bryn y Fedwen	Pumlumon
180	Carling Knott	Great Gable
181	Disgwylfa	Brecon Beacons
182	Featherbed Top	Peak District
183	Mill Hill	Peak District
184	White Hill	Bowland Forest
185	Foel Benddin	Arans
186	Yarnspath Law	Cheviots
187	Black Chew Head	Peak District
188	Gwaunceste Hill	Radnor Forest
189	Gyrn	Carneddau
190	West Fell	Great Shunner
191	Garn Gron	Rhayader
192	Lank Rigg	Great Gable
193	Lord's Seat	Peak District
194	Mynydd Bryn-llech	Arenigs
195	Bolt's Law	Burnhope Seat
196	Brown Clee Hill	Long Mynd

Height in Metres	Date Ascended/Notes
547	_____
547	_____
547	_____
546	_____
546	_____
546	_____
546	_____
546	_____
546	_____
545+	_____
545	_____
545	_____
545	_____
545	_____
544	_____
544	_____
544	_____
544	_____
544	_____
544	_____
544	_____
543	_____
543	_____
542	_____
542	_____
542	_____
542	_____
541	_____
541	_____
540+	_____
540+	_____
540	_____
540	_____

Top No	Name	Group
197	Rhialgwm	Berwyns
198	Cuns Fell	Cross Fell
199	Craig Dyfnant	Rhayader
200	Ffordd Gefn	Berwyns
201	Rhiwaedog-uwch-afon	Arans
202	Back Tor	Peak District
203	Carnedd Lago	Arenigs
204	Castle Knott	Ingleborough
205	Cerrig Gwaun-y-llan	Rhayader
206	Drum Ddu	Rhayader
207	Esgair y Llwyn	Rhayader
208	Great Mis Tor	Dartmoor
209	Llechwedd Hirgoed - West	Pumlumon
210	Nyth-grug	Radnor Forest
211	Parson's Pulpit	Ingleborough
212	Banc Dolwen	Rhayader
213	Calf Crag	Scafell
214	Graig Ddu	Arenigs
215	Great Mell Fell	Helvellyn
216	Newton Tors	Cheviots
217	Foel Cwmcerwyn	Preseli
218	Foel-ganol	Carneddau
219	Stiperstones	Long Mynd
220	Blea Moor	Ingleborough
221	Harland Hill	Ingleborough
222	Llechwedd Hirgoed	Pumlumon
223	Mynydd Ton	Brecon Beacons
224	Whin Rigg	Scafell
225	Mynydd Mawr	Berwyns
226	Esgair Penygarreg	Rhayader
227	Garn Prŷs	Arenigs
228	Titterstone Clee Hill	Long Mynd
229	Colva Hill	Radnor Forest

Height in Metres	*Date Ascended/Notes*
540	
539	_____
539	_____
539	_____
539	_____
538	_____
538	_____
538	_____
538	_____
538	_____
538	_____
538	_____
538	_____
538	_____
538	_____
537	_____
537	_____
537	_____
537	_____
537	_____
536	_____
536	_____
536	_____
535	_____
535	_____
535	_____
535	_____
535	_____
534	_____
533	_____
533	_____
533	_____
532	_____

Top No	Name	Group
230	Hamel Down	Dartmoor
231	Mwdwl-eithin	Hiraethog
232	Mynydd Maes-glas	Arans
233	Uldale Head	Great Shunner
234	Hatterrall Hill	Black Mountains
235	High Wether Howe	High Street
236	Proctor High Mark	Ingleborough
237	Carn Pen-rhiw-ddu	Brecon Beacons
238	Mynydd Nodal	Arenigs
239	Dibyn Du	Rhayader
240	White Howe	High Street
241	Caw	Coniston
242	Foel Fras	Pumlumon
243	Foel Grafiau	Pumlumon
244	Moel Hyddgen	Pumlumon
245	Cilfaesty Hill	Radnor Forest
246	Foel Fawr	Arenigs
247	The Forest	High Street
248	Gors Lydan	Radnor Forest
249	Mynydd Blaengwynfi	Brecon Beacons
250	Shill Moor	Cheviots
251	Cefn y Cnwc	Rhayader
252	Higher White Tor	Dartmoor
253	Pen y Bedw	Moelwyns
254	Ravens Knowe	Cheviots
255	Wolfhole Crag	Bowland Forest
256	Esgair Ganol	Rhayader
257	Gavel Fell	Great Gable
258	Great Cockup	Skiddaw
259	High Snockrigg	Buttermere
260	Preston Hill	Cheviots
261	Crug Gynon	Rhayader
262	Pike Rigg	Burnhope Seat

Height in Metres	Date Ascended/Notes
532	_____
532	_____
532	_____
532	_____
531	_____
531	_____
531	_____
530+	_____
530+	_____
530	_____
530	_____
529	_____
529	_____
529	_____
529	_____
528	_____
528	_____
528	_____
528	_____
528	_____
528	_____
527	_____
527	_____
527	_____
527	_____
527	_____
526	_____
526	_____
526	_____
526	_____
526	_____
525	_____
525	_____

Top No	Name	Group
263	Whinlatter	Buttermere
264	Ayle Common	Burnhope Seat
265	High House Fell	High Street
266	Moel Dyrnogydd	Moelwyns
267	Carnedd Wen	Arans
268	Crag Fell	Great Gable
269	Craig yr Hafod	Arenigs
270	Gyrn Moelfre	Berwyns
271	Glascwm Hill	Radnor Forest
272	Great How	Scafell
273	Gyrn Ddu	Moel Hebog
274	High Greygrits	Great Shunner
275	Moelfryn	Rhayader
276	Souther Fell	Skiddaw
277	Carnedd Dâs Eithin	Berwyns
278	Harter Fell	Great Shunner
279	Moel Hen-fache	Berwyns
280	Moel y Gydros	Arenigs
281	Moel y Llyn	Pumlumon
282	Banc Bwlchygarreg	Pumlumon
283	Bryn-pig	Arenig
284	Cats Tor	Peak District
285	Fair Snape Fell	Bowland Forest
286	Moel Cae'r-defaid	Arenigs
287	Moudy Mea	Great Shunner
288	Pen Lan-fawr	Rhayader
289	Rhobell Ganol	Arenigs
290	Brownber Hill	Cross Fell
291	Bryn Banog	Moel Hebog
292	Craig Dolfudr - North Top	Arenigs
293	Dunkery Beacon	Exmoor
294	Foel Gôch	Hiraethog
295	Horseshoe Hill	Burnhope Seat

Height in Metres	*Date Ascended/Notes*
525	_____
524	_____
524	_____
524	_____
523	_____
523	_____
523	_____
523	_____
522	_____
522	_____
522	_____
522	_____
522	_____
522	_____
521	_____
521	_____
521	_____
521	_____
521	_____
520+	_____
520+	_____
520+	_____
520+	_____
520+	_____
520+	_____
520+	_____
520+	_____
519	_____
519	_____
519	_____
519	_____
519	_____
519	_____

Top No	Name	Group
296	Bryn Coch	Radnor Forest
297	Craig Dolfudr	Arenigs
298	Gorsedd Brân	Hiraethog
299	Moel Morwynion	Rhinogs
300	Sighty Crag	Cheviots
301	Broadhope Hill	Cheviots
302	Cyrniau y Llyn	Berwyns
303	Lad Law	South Pennines
304	Mam Tor	Peak District
305	Mynydd Egryn	Rhinogs
306	Mynydd Trawsnant	Rhayader
307	North Hessary Tor	Dartmoor
308	Collier Law	Burnhope Seat
309	Great Knipe	Cross Fell
310	The Long Mynd	Long Mynd
311	Pool Hill	Radnor Forest
312	Sallows	High Street
313	Hirwaun Common	Brecon Beacons
314	Mynydd Llangorse	Black Mountains
315	Ryder's Hill	Dartmoor
316	Glendhu Hill	Cheviots
317	Mynydd Fron-fraith	Cadair Idris
318	Pen Foel-y-ffridd	Arans
319	Allt Forgan	Brecon Beacons
320	Corndon Hill	Long Mynd
321	Monkside	Cheviots
322	Oliver Hill	Peak District
323	Mellbreak	Great Gable
324	Pen Trum-gwr	Cadair Idris
325	Bryn-mawr	Arenigs
326	Eglwyseg Mountain	Clwydian Hills
327	Foel Fenlli	Clwydian Hills
328	Garn Wen	Rhayader

Height in Metres	Date Ascended/Notes
518	_____
518	_____
518	_____
518	_____
518	_____
517	_____
517	_____
517	_____
517	_____
517	_____
517	_____
517	_____
516	_____
516	_____
516	_____
516	_____
516	_____
515	_____
515	_____
515	_____
514	_____
514	_____
514	_____
513	_____
513	_____
513	_____
513	_____
512	_____
512	_____
511	_____
511	_____
511	_____
511	_____

Top No	Name	Group
329	Manod Bach	Moelwyns
330	Park Fell	Black Fell
331	Penrhiw-wen	Rhayader
332	Clee Burf	Long Mynd
333	Lint Lands	Cheviots
334	Beda Head	High Street
335	Bwlch Mawr	Moel Hebog
336	Camlo Hill	Rhayader
337	Gopa Uchaf	Rhayader
338	Hen Comb	Great Gable
339	Mellbreak - North Top	Great Gable
340	Red Hill	Radnor Forest
341	Twynwalter	Brecon Beacons
342	Brondre-fawr Hill	Rhayader
343	Brownhart Law	Cheviots
344	Godre Fynydd	Cadair Idris
345	Sychnentydd	Rhayader
346	Black Edge	Peak District
347	Disgwylfa Fawr	Pumlumon
348	Pen Creigiau'r Llan	Pumlumon
349	Warren Hill	Radnor Forest
350	Burnsall and Thorpe Fell	Ingleborough
351	Shutlingsloe	Peak District
352	White Ridge	Dartmoor
353	Coed Nant-yr-hwch	Rhayader
354	Little Mell Fell	Helvellyn
355	Moel Hywel	Rhayader
356	The Roaches	Peak District
357	Moel y Gaer	Clwydian Hills
358	Rhobell-y-big	Arenigs
359	Y Domen Fawr	Brecon Beacons
360	Cam Rakes	Ingleborough
361	Moel Oernant	Arenigs

Height in Metres	Date Ascended/Notes
511	
511	
510+	
510	
510	
509	
509	
509	
509	
509	
509	
509	
509	
508	
508	
508	
508	
507	
507	
507	
507	
506	
506	
506	
505	
505	
505	
505	
504	
504	
504	
503	
503	

Top No	Name	Group
362	Craig Bron-banog	Hiraethog
363	Dodd	Skiddaw
364	Moel Gamallt	Moelwyns
365	Mynydd Ynyscorrwg	Brecon Beacons
366	High Dodd	High Street
367	Hungry Law	Cheviots
368	Shillhope Law	Cheviots
369	Banc yr Wyn	Pumlumon
370	Esgair Berfa	Cadair Idris
371	Carraghan	Isle of Man
372	Ffridd yr Allt-llŵyd	Arenigs
373	West Nab	Peak District

Height in Metres	Date Ascended/Notes
502	_____
502	_____
502	_____
502	_____
501	_____
501	_____
501	_____
500+	_____
500+	_____
500	_____
500	_____
500	_____

Table of the 500-Metre Tops in Alphabetical Order

Name	Top No
Allt Forgan	319
Alston Moor	64
Amicombe Hill	56
Angletarn Pikes	92
Arant Haw	11
Ard Crags	63
Axe Edge	152
Axe Edge Moor	138
Aye Gill Pike	123
Ayle Common	264
Back Tor	202
Banc Bugeilyn	139
Banc Bwlchygarreg	282
Banc Dolwen	212
Banc Llechwedd-mawr	112
Banc yr Wyn	369
Beacon Hill	163
Beda Head	334
Beefstand Hill	106
Beinn-y-phott	178
Bessyboot	159
Black Chew Head	187
Black Combe	26
Black Edge	346
Black Hag	153
Black Hill	60
Blaen Rhestr	164
Blake Fell	75
Blea Moor	220
Bleaberry Fell	43
Blorenge	110
Blotting Raise	40
Bolt's Law	195

Name	*Top No*
Braich Ddu	167
Broadhope Hill	301
Brondre-fawr Hill	342
Brown Clee Hill	196
Brown Haw	57
Brown Knoll	85
Brownber Hill	290
Brownhart Law	343
Bryn	107
Bryn Banog	291
Bryn Coch	296
Bryn Du	108
Bryn Glâs	116
Bryn y Fedwen	179
Bryn-mawr	325
Bryn-pig	283
Buck Barrow	154
Burnsall and Thorpe Fell	350
Bwlch Mawr	335
Calf Crag	213
Calf Top	1
Cam Rakes	360
Camlo Hill	336
Carling Knott	180
Carn Pen-rhiw-ddu	237
Carnedd Dâs Eithin	277
Carnedd Lago	203
Carnedd Wen	267
Carnedd y Cribau	41
Carraghan	371
Carreg Goch	117
Carter Fell - North	66
Castle Knott	204

Name	Top No
Name	*Top No*
Cats Tor	284
Caw	241
Cefn Coch	80
Cefn Croes	76
Cefn y Cnwc	251
Cefn y Cylchau	124
Cefnffordd	27
Ceiswyn	174
Cerrig Coediog	39
Cerrig Gwaun-y-llan	205
Cilfaesty Hill	245
Clagh Ouyr	140
Clagh Ouyr - North Top	146
Clee Burf	332
Coed Nant-yr-hwch	353
Collier Law	308
Colva Hill	229
Corndon Hill	320
Cosdon Hill	147
Cosh Knott	21
Crag Fell	268
Craig Bron-banog	362
Craig Ddrwg	32
Craig Dolfudr	297
Craig Dolfudr - North Top	292
Craig Dyfnant	199
Craig Portas	12
Craig Portas - East Top	50
Craig Wen	160
Craig Wion	93
Craig y Grut	45
Craig yr Hafod	269
Crug Gynon	261
Crugyn Llwyd	81
Cuns Fell	198

Name	*Top No*
Cut Hill	18
Cyrn-y-Brain	96
Cyrniau y Llyn	302
Dead Man's Hill	168
Deadwater Fell	82
Dibyn Du	239
Disgwylfa	181
Disgwylfa Fawr	347
Dodd	363
Draws Drum	84
Drosgol	148
Drum Ddu	206
Dry Rigg	95
Drybedd	94
Dunkery Beacon	293
Dunmoor Hill	86
Eglwyseg Mountain	326
Esgair Berfa	370
Esgair Ganol	256
Esgair Penygarreg	226
Esgair y Llwyn	207
Fair Snape Fell	285
Featherbed Top	182
Ffordd Gefn	200
Ffrîdd yr Allt-llŵyd	372
Foel Benddin	185
Foel Cwmcerwyn	217
Foel Fadian	101
Foel Fawr	246
Foel Fenlli	327
Foel Figenau	44
Foel Fraith	22
Foel Fras	242
Foel Goch (Snowdon)	13
Foel Gôch (Hiraethog)	294

Name	Top No
Foel Grafiau	243
Foel Lwyd	19
Foel Uchaf	97
Foel-boeth	33
Foel-ganol	218
Forest The	247
Fron-wen	169
Garn Gron	191
Garn Prŷs	227
Garn Wen	328
Garnedd Fawr	87
Gavel Fell	257
Geifas	78
Glan-hafon	7
Glascwm Hill	271
Glendhu Hill	316
Godre Fynydd	344
Gopa Uchaf	337
Gors Lydan	248
Gorsedd Brân	298
Graig Ddu	214
Graig Goch	52
Graig Wen	125
Great Cockup	258
Great How	272
Great Knipe	309
Great Links Tor	53
Great Mell Fell	215
Great Mis Tor	208
Great Pinseat	59
Green Bell	14
Grizdales	129
Gwastad	141
Gwaunceste Hill	188
Gyrn	189

Name	*Top No*
Gyrn Ddu	273
Gyrn Moelfre	270
Hamel Down	230
Hangingstone Hill	20
Hard Knott	155
Hard Rigg	170
Harland Hill	221
Harter Fell (Great Shunner)	278
Hatterrall Hill	234
Haystacks	30
Hazelgill Knott	67
Height of Hazely	130
Hen Comb	338
High Dodd	366
High Greygrits	274
High House Fell	266
High Seat	8
High Snockrigg	259
High Wether Howe	235
Higher White Tor	252
Hirwaun Common	313
Hooksey	54
Hoove	131
Horse Head Moor	2
Horseshoe Hill	295
Howden Edge	149
Hungry Law	367
Illgill Head	3
Iron Band	103
Kensgriff	74
Knott Rigg	126
Lad Law	303
Lank Rigg	192
Lint Lands	333
Little Mell Fell	354

Name	Top No
Little Whernside	15
Llechwedd Ddu	113
Llechwedd Hirgoed	222
Llechwedd Hirgoed - West Top	209
Long Mynd The	310
Lord's Seat (Buttermere)	135
Lord's Seat (Peak District)	193
Mam Tor	304
Manod Bach	329
Mellbreak	323
Mellbreak - North Top	339
Meugher	73
Middle Fell	61
Mill Hill	183
Moel Cae'r-defaid	286
Moel Dyrnogydd	266
Moel Eilio	171
Moel Emoel	156
Moel Eunant	89
Moel Fammau	128
Moel Farlwyd	69
Moel Feity	42
Moel Gamallt	364
Moel Hen-fache	279
Moel Hyddgen	244
Moel Hywel	355
Moel Llygoed	29
Moel Meirch	9
Moel Morfydd	157
Moel Morwynion	299
Moel Oernant	361
Moel Wnion	65
Moel Ymenyn	150
Moel y Faen	161
Moel y Feidiog	70

Name	*Top No*
Moel y Gaer	357
Moel y Gamelin	71
Moel y Gydros	280
Moel y Llyn	281
Moel y Pawl	10
Moel yr Henfaes	58
Moelfre	46
Moelfryn	275
Moel-ddu	132
Monkside	321
Moudy Mea	287
Murton Pike	35
Mwdwl-eithin	231
Mynydd Blaengwynfi	249
Mynydd Braich-gôch	31
Mynydd Bryn-llech	194
Mynydd Caerau	127
Mynydd Carn-y-cefn	151
Mynydd Coch	88
Mynydd Coety	68
Mynydd Egryn	305
Mynydd Fron-fraith	317
Mynydd Graig Goch	4
Mynydd Llangorse	314
Mynydd Llanynidr	120
Mynydd Maes-glas	232
Mynydd Mawr (Berwyns)	225
Mynydd Nodal	238
Mynydd Ton	223
Mynydd Trawsnant	306
Mynydd Troed	5
Mynydd Tywi	162
Mynydd Tywi - East Top	175
Mynydd Ynyscorrwg	365
Nab The	72

Name	Top No
Nateby Common	165
Naughtberry Hill	77
Newton Tors	216
North Barrule	98
North Hessary Tor	307
Nyth-grug	210
Oliver Hill	322
Outerside	90
Pant y Creigiau	99
Pant-llwyd	158
Park Fell	330
Parson's Pulpit	211
Peel Fell	23
Pegwn Mawr	55
Pen Creigiau'r Llan	348
Pen Foel-y-ffridd	318
Pen Lan-fawr	288
Pen Trum-gwr	324
Pen y Bedw	253
Pendle Hill	121
Penrhiw-wen	331
Pickerstone Ridge	100
Pike Rigg	262
Pool Hill	311
Preston Hill	260
Proctor High Mark	236
Ravens Knowe	254
Red Hill	340
Redshaw Moss	176
Rhialgwm	197
Rhiwaedog-uwch-afon	201
Rhobell Ganol	289
Rhobell-y-big	358
Rhwng y Ddwynant	48
Roaches The	356

Name	*Top No*
Roman Fell	36
Ryder's Hill	315
Rye Loaf Hill	166
Sallows	312
Schil The	25
Sergeant's Crag	83
Shill Moor	250
Shillhope Law	368
Shining Tor	114
Shutlingsloe	351
Siambr Trawsfynydd	62
Sighty Crag	300
Simon's Seat	51
Souther Fell	276
Steel Fell	133
Stiperstones	219
Swinglebank Crag	134
Sychnentydd	345
Tarn Seat	142
Tarren Cwm-ffernol	144
Thack Moor	6
Thirl Moor	118
Tir Riwiog	177
Titterstone Clee Hill	228
Tor y Foel	143
Twyn Crugyrafan	122
Twynwalter	341
Uldale Head	233
Vivod Mountain	145
Ward's Stone	111
Warren Hill	349
Waun Claerddu	37
Waun Leuci	109
Werfa	91
West Fell	190

Name	*Top No*
West Nab	373
Wether Cairn	104
Whetstone Ridge	173
Whimble	28
Whin Rigg	224
Whinlatter	263
White Hill	184
White Howe	240
White Ridge	352
Whitfell	79
Wold Fell	119
Wolfhole Crag	255
Wool Meath	136
Y Domen Fawr	359
Y Fawnen	105
Y Foel	172
Y Gamallt	49
Y Gamriw	16
Y Garnedd	137
Y Gribin	24
Y Ro Wen	38
Yarnspath Law	186
Yr Allt	17
Yr Arddu	47
Yr Eifl	102
Yr Orsedd	115
Y-fâl or Sugar Loaf	34

ANALYSIS OF THE 500-METRE TOPS BY GROUPS AND AREAS

Area	Group	No of Tops
Lake District:	1. Scafell	10
	2. Great Gable	10
	3. Buttermere	6
	4. Skiddaw	3
	5. Helvellyn	2
	6. High Street	10
	7. Coniston	4
	Total	**45**
Rest of England:	8. Cheviots	23
	9. Black Fell	3
	10. Cross Fell	6
	11. Burnhope Seat	8
	12. Great Shunner	16
	13. Ingleborough	21
	14. Forest of Bowland	4
	15. South Pennines	2
	16. Peak District	19
	17. Long Mynd	5*
	* Not Including 1 top in Wales	
	18. Exmoor	1
	19. Dartmoor	11
	Total	**119**
North Wales:	20. Carneddau	7
	21. Clwydian Hills	8
	22. Hiraethog	4
	23. Snowdon	1
	24. Moel Hebog	6
	25. Moelwyns	11
	26. Arenigs	23
	27. Rhinogs	6
	28. Arans	13
	29. Berwyns	13
	30. Cadair Idris	11
	Total	**103**

Area	*Group*	*No of Tops*
Mid & South Wales:	31. Pumlumon	19
	32. Long Mynd	1
	33. Rhayader	35
	34. Radnor Forest	13
	35. Black Mountains	4
	36. Brecon Beacons	28
	37. Preseli	1
	Total	**101**
	38. Isle of Man	5
Grand Totals:	England	164
	Wales	204
	Total + IOM	**373**

Breakdown by height bands

600 - 610m	27
575 - 599m	46
550 - 574m	78
525 - 549m	113
500 - 524m	109
Total	**373**

Chapter 3

Notable Hill Tops of England and Wales

INTRODUCTION

Following my investigations into the 2000s and 500s of England and Wales, I decided that a list of hills of lesser altitude would be of value. Much of the population of this country live some distance from mountains and moorlands, and for those hill walkers I have compiled a list of major hills and downs. The Landranger maps formed the basis and I refined the list by visiting the Ordnance Survey Headquarters at Southampton, where I had access to the more detailed Pathfinder maps.

I have called this table the Notable Hill Tops and I hope that the information provided will prove useful for those living in lowland areas. I have not provided a strict definition of what constitutes a notable hill, using instead an element of judgement when deciding if a top is worthy of inclusion. In my view a hill top should be a high point on a hill or downland area with potential for a country walk. This is, to my knowledge, the first published list of this type and in time it could probably be refined.

Notable Hill Groups

1. Berwick upon Tweed
2. Cheviots
3. Simonside Hills
4. Hadrian's Wall
5. North York Moors
6. Yorkshire Wolds
7. Howardian Hills
8. Ingleborough
9. North Yorkshire
10. Forest of Bowland
11. South Pennines
12. Lincolnshire Wolds
13. Lincolnshire Edge
14. Peak District
15. Peckforton Hills
16. Norfolk
17. Cannock Chase
18. Charnwood Forest
19. Long Mynd
20. Clent Hills
21. Lickey Hills
22. Malvern Hills
23. Cotswolds
24. Forest of Dean
25. Chilterns
26. Lambourn Downs
27. Marlborough Downs
28. Berkshire Downs
29. London
30. Hampshire Downs
31. Mendips
32. Salisbury Plain
33. North Down
34. Lundy Island
35. Quantock Hills
36. Brendon Hills
37. Exmoor
38. Blackdown Hills
39. Cranborne Chase
40. Dorset Chalk Hills
41. South Downs
42. Surrey
43. The Weald
44. Dartmoor
45. Devon
46. Purbeck Hills
47. Isle of Wight
48. Bodmin Moor
49. St Austell Moors
50. West Penwith Moors
51. Carn Menellis Moor
52. Goonhilly Downs
53. Isle of Scilly
54. Anglesea
55. Clwydian Hills
56. Lleyn Peninsular
57. Breidden Hills
58. Preseli
59. Radnor Forest
60. Mynydd Eppynt
61. Black Mountains
62. Gower Peninsular

Hadrian's Wall (*Author*)

TABLE OF THE NOTABLE HILL TOPS IN GROUP ORDER

Top No	Name	Height in	
		Metres	Feet

1. Berwick upon Tweed

315	Halidon Hill	163	534

Notes   1. The most northerly hill in England

2. Cheviots

128	Hepburn Moor	315	1033

Notes1. Summit is named Ross Castle Fort

3. Simonside Hills

38	Tosson Hill	440	1443
44	Simonside	430	1410
60	Gunner's Box	407	1335

4. Hadrian's Wall

111	Melkridge Common	345	1131

Notes   1. Highest point on Hadrian's Wall

Grid Reference	Ordnance Map 1/50k	1/25k	Notes
969548	75	438	1.
081253	75	476	1.
005982	81	511	
024987	81	511	
987965	81	510	
742676	86/87	545	1.

Top No	Name	Height in Metres	Feet

5. North York Moors

Top No	Name	Metres	Feet
25	Round Hill	454	1489
41	Stony Ridge	434	1423
42	Cringle Moor	432	1417
43	Danby High Moor	432	1417
45	Rosedale Head	429	1407
62	Noon Hill	404	1325
68	Black Hambleton	400	1312
72	White Hill	398	1305
81	Cold Moor	385	1263
84	Blakey Ridge	383	1256
88	Golden Heights	376	1233
89	Little Moor	374	1227
102	Coal Hill	360	1181
120	Helmsley Bank	328	1076
121	Hob on the Hill	328	1076
124	Roseberry Topping	320	1049
131	High Barn	313	1026
144	Stony Leas	299	980
146	Sutton Bank	298	977

Notes
1. Cleveland Hills
2. Summit is named Drake How
3. Also named Seavey Hill
4. Also named Westerdale Moor
5. Also named Rudland Rigg
6. Cleveland county top
7. Hambleton Hills

Grid Reference	Ordnance Map 1/50k	1/25k	Notes
594016	93	26	1.
632028	94	26	
538029	93	26	2.
702012	94	26	3.
673018	93	26	4.
540988	100	26	1.
481946	100	26	
566037	93	26	1.
552019	93	26	
686980	94/100	26	
650955	94/100	26	5.
489904	100	26	
506991	100	26	1.
588906	100	26	
635123	94	26	6.
579126	94	26	1.
508867	100	26	7.
887992	94/101	27	
518824	100	26	7.

Top No	Name	Height in Metres	Feet

6. Yorkshire Wolds

Top No	Name	Metres	Feet
214	Cot Nab	246	807
227	Birdsall Brow	237	777
296	Heslerton Wold	190	623
305	Staxton Wold	178	583
308	Potter Brompton Wold	176	577

Notes   1. Humberside county top

7. Howardian Hills

310	Yearsley Moor	174	570

8. Ingleborough

5	Simon's Seat	485	1591

9. North Yorkshire

142	Brimham Rocks	301	987

Notes   1. Also named Brimham Moor

10. Forest of Bowland

77	Waddington Fell	395	1295

Grid Reference	Ordnance Map		Notes
	1/50k	1/25k	
821570	106	666	1.
815628	100	656	
923750	101	644	
021778	101	645	
986761	101	644	
597744	100	642	
079598	104	10	
206651	99	653	1.
715475	103	669	

Top No	Name	Height in Metres	Feet

11. South Pennines

Top No	Name	Metres	Feet
7	Hoofe Stones Height	479	1571
10	Top of Leach	474	1555
12	Blackstone Edge	472	1548
15	Birkin Clough Head	465+	1525+
22	Winter Hill	456	1496
24	Round Hill	455+	1492+
26	Trough Edge End	454	1489
27	Dick Delf Hill	452	1482
28	Nab Hill	451	1479
29	Thieveley Pike	449	1473
30	White Hill	446	1463
34	Wolf Stones	443	1453
35	Carr and Crags Moor	441	1446
39	Dog Hill	435	1427
52	Bull Hill	418	1371
53	Manshead End	417	1368
58	Great Hameldon	409	1341
65	Rombald's Moor	402	1318
66	Stoodley Pike	402	1318
69	Brown Wardle Hill	400	1312

Notes   1. Also named Black Hameldon
              2. Summit is named Robin Hood's Bed
              3. Also named Deerplay Moor
              4. Also named Holcombe Moor

Grid Reference	Ordnance Map 1/50k	1/25k	Notes
914291	103	21	1.
851195	109	701	
972164	109	21	2.
919325	103	21	
660149	109	700	
978350	103	21	
906219	103	21	
984348	103	21	
037323	104	21	
872271	103	21	3.
007313	104	21	
971394	103	21	
894251	103	21	
003171	110	21	
767187	109	700	4.
998198	109	21	
794289	103	689	
115453	104	671	5.
974241	103	21	6.
898187	109	21	

5. Also named Ilkley Moor
6. Site of Napoleonic Monument

| Top No | Name | Height in | |
| | | Metres | Feet |

12. Lincolnshire Wolds

Top No	Name	Metres	Feet
312	Normaby-le-wold	168	551
318	High Street	149	488
327	Saxby Wolds	102	334
328	Somerby Top	97	318

Notes   1. Lincolnshire county top

13. Lincolnshire Edge

| 325 | Leadenham Heath | 105+ | 344+ |

Grid Reference	Ordnance Map 1/50k	1/25k	Notes
121964	113	730	1.
178898	113	747	
999173	112	706	
069073	112	719	
961514	121	797	

Top No	Name	Height in Metres	Feet

14. Peak District

Top No	Name	Metres	Feet
9	Lose Hill	476	1561
18	Winhill Pike	462	1515
20	High Neb	458	1502
23	Ramshaw Rocks	455+	1492+
50	High Wheeldon	422	1384
54	Durham Edge	416	1364
57	Hen Cloud	410	1345
67	Sutton Common	402	1318
80	Wolfscote Hill	388	1272
82	Gun	385	1263
90	Beeley Moor	371	1217
93	Weaver Hill	371	1217
95	Ecton Hill	369	1210
97	White Edge	366	1200
104	Wetton Hill	358	1174
106	Soles Hill	355	1164
112	The Cloud	343	1125
132	Kerridge Hill	313	1026

Notes
1. Also named Ward's Piece
2. Also named Win Hill
3. Also named Abney Moor
4. Also named Croker Hill
5. Also named Throwley Moor

15. Peckforton Hills

Top No	Name	Metres	Feet
244	Raw Head	227	744
264	Maiden Castle	212	695

Notes
1. Also named Bickerton Hill

Grid Reference	Ordnance Map 1/50k	1/25k	Notes
153854	110	1	1.
187851	110	1	2.
228853	110	743	
020625	119	24	
100661	119	24	
181794	119	24	3.
009616	119	24	
934676	118	24	4.
137583	119	24	
970615	118	24	
293687	119	24	
095464	119/128	810	
100580	119	24	
260764	119	24	
105562	119	24	
098525	119	24	5.
905637	118	776	
942759	118	759	
508548	117	790	1.
497529	117	790	

Top No	Name	Height in Metres	Feet

16. Norfolk

| 332 | Ongar Hill | 4 | 13 |

Notes   1. England's lowest hill, a hamlet not a hill!

17. Cannock Chase

| 222 | Castle Hill | 242 | 793 |

Notes   1. Site of hill fort

18. Charnwood Forest

| 167 | Bardon Hill | 279 | 915 |
| 207 | Beacon Hill | 248 | 813 |

Notes   1. Leicestershire county top

Grid Reference	Ordnance Map 1/50k	1/25k	Notes
579246	131	858	1.
043128	128	872	1.
460132	129	874	1.
509148	129	874	

Top No	Name	Height in Metres	Feet

19. Long Mynd

Top No	Name	Metres	Feet
19	Caer Caradoc Hill	459	1505
59	Long Mountain	408	1338
61	The Wrekin	407	1335
71	Ragleth Hill	398	1305
79	Hope Bowdler Hill	393	1289
87	The Lawley	377	1236
94	Roundton	370	1213
115	Callow Hill	335+	1099+
123	Earl's Hill	320	1049
127	Diddlebury Common	317	1040
164	Wenlock Edge	280+	918+

Notes 1. Summit is named Beacon Ring, site of hill fort
       2. Also named Pontesford Hill, site of hill fort

20. Clent Hills

Top No	Name	Metres	Feet
130	Walton Hill	315	1033
135	Adam's Hill	309	1013

21. Lickey Hills

Top No	Name	Metres	Feet
145	Beacon Hill	298	977
159	Waseley Hill	287	941

Notes 1. Also named Chapman's Hill

| Grid Reference | Ordnance Map | | Notes |
	1/50k	1/25k	
478954	137/138	910	
265058	126	888	1.
628081	127	890	
454921	137/138	910	
483937	137/138	910	
495975	137/138	910	
294950	137	909	
461851	137/138	931	
409048	126	889	2.
483868	137/138	931	
513906	137/138	910	
943798	139	953	
937805	139	933	
987760	139	953	
972779	139	953	1.

Top No	Name	Height in Metres	Feet

22. Malvern Hills

Top No	Name	Metres	Feet
48	Worcester Beacon	425	1394
73	North Hill	397	1302
114	Hereford Beacon	338	1108
160	Midsummer Hill	286	938
295	Chase End Hill	191	626

Note   1. Site of hill fort

23. Cotswolds

Top No	Name	Metres	Feet
118	Cleeve Hill	330	1082
125	Broadway Hill	319	1046
143	Bredon Hill	299	980
147	Birdlip Hill	297	974
153	Leckhampton Hill	293	961
163	Painswick Beacon	283	928
174	Crickley Hill	273	895
190	Ilmington Down	261	856
198	Haresfield Hill	256	839
237	Brailes Hill	232	761
240	Dover's Hill	230	754
275	Nibley Knoll	203	666
290	Meon Hill	194	636

Notes   1. Gloucestershire county top
             2. Also named Painswick Hill, site of hill fort
             3. Site of Country Park and hill fort
             4. Warwickshire county top, also named Ebrington Hill
             5. Also named Scottsquar Hill
             6. Summit is named Highwall Spinney
             7. Site of Tyndale Monument

Grid Reference	Ordnance Map 1/50k	1/25k	Notes
769452	150	1018	
769464	150	1018	
760400	150	1018	1.
759375	150	1041	1.
761355	150	1041	
997246	163	1066	1.
115348	150	1043	
957403	150	1019	
926141	163	1089	
949184	163	1089	
868121	162	1089	2.
932164	163	1089	3.
188426	151	1020	4.
837086	162	1113	5.
295390	151	1044	6.
137396	151	1043	
746956	172	1132	7.
176453	151	1020	

Top No	Name	Height in Metres	Feet

24. Forest of Dean

Top No	Name	Metres	Feet
149	May Hill	296	971
156	Ruardean Hill	290	951
168	Buck Stone	279	915
206	Kymin	250+	820+
281	Coppet Hill	200+	656+

Notes   1. Site of Naval Temple

25. Chilterns

Top No	Name	Metres	Feet
182	Aston Hill	267	875
192	Coombe Hill	260	853
197	Bald Hill	257	843
210	Pulpit Hill	248	813
219	Wain Hill	244	800
220	Dunstable Down	243	797
239	Beacon Hill	230	754
286	Muswell Hill	198	649
298	Quainton Hill	187	613

Notes   1. Buckinghamshire county top
           2. Oxfordshire county top
           3. Site of hill fort
           4. Bedfordshire county top
           5. Also named Ivenhoe Beacon, site of hill fort
           6. Hill located 9 miles NW of Chilterns ridge

Grid Reference	Ordnance Map 1/50k	1/25k	Notes
696213	162	1065	
636169	162	14	
542123	162	14	
528124	162	14	1.
578182	162	14	
890090	165	1118	1.
849068	165	1118	
729958	165	1137	2.
832051	165	1118	3.
774008	165	1117	
009194	166	1095	4.
960169	165	1094	5.
641153	165	1093	6.
751213	165	1070	6.

Top No	Name	Height in Metres	Feet

26. Lambourn Downs

Top No	Name	Metres	Feet
191	Uffington Hill	261	856
200	Charlbury Hill	253	830
218	Sparshalt Down	244	800
243	Crowberry Tump	227	744

Notes   1. Also named Whitehorse Hill, site of hill fort
           2. Also named Weathercock Hill

27. Marlborough Downs

Top No	Name	Metres	Feet
151	Milk Hill	294	964
152	Tan Hill	294	964
157	Martinsell Hill	289	948
170	Liddington Hill	277	908
176	Hackpen Hill	272	892
178	Golden Ball Hill	270+	885+
180	Barbury Hill	268	879
193	Morgan's Hill	260	853
195	Cherhill Down	258	846
213	Coombe Down	246	807

Notes   1. Wiltshire county top
           2. Site of hill fort
           3. Site of monument and hill fort

Grid Reference	Ordnance Map 1/50k	1/25k	Notes
301864	174	1154	1.
238821	174	1154	
337851	174	1154	
285827	174	1154	2.
104641	173	1185	1.
082647	173	1185	1.
178639	173	1185	2.
210798	174	1170	2.
129744	173	1169	
129640	173	1185	
154762	173	1169	2.
030669	173	1185	
049694	173	1185	3.
182745	173	1169	

Top No	Name	Height in Metres	Feet

28. Berkshire Downs

Top No	Name	Metres	Feet
274	Cuckhamsley Hill	203	666
300	Lowbury Hill	186	611

Notes   1. Also named Fore Down

29. London

Top No	Name	Metres	Feet
329	Barn Hill	86	282
330	Horsendon Hill	85	278

30. Hampshire Downs

Top No	Name	Metres	Feet
148	Walbury Hill	297	974
154	Inkpen Hill	290+	951+
161	Pilot Hill	286	938
188	Beacon Hill	261	856
196	Haydown Hill	258	846
203	Little Down	252	826
230	Watership Down	237	777
238	Ladle Hill	232	761
321	Danebury Hill	143	469

Notes   1. Berkshire county top, site of hill fort
             2. Hampshire county top
             3. Site of hill fort

Grid Reference	Ordnance Map		Notes
	1/50k	1/25k	
456851	174	1155	1.
540823	174	1155	
193874	176	1158	
162844	176	1158	
374616	174	1186	1.
356619	174	1186	
399601	174	1186	2.
458573	174	1203	3.
314566	174	1186	
308554	185	1202	
495568	174	1203	
479568	174	1203	3.
323377	185	1242	3.

Top No	Name	Height in Metres	Feet

31. Mendips

Top No	Name	Metres	Feet
122	Beacon Batch	325	1066
140	North Hill	307	1007
141	Pen Hill	305	1000
216	Callow Hill	245+	803+
235	Dundry Hill	233	764
253	Small Down Knoll	222	728
267	Wavering Down	211	692
284	Creech Hill	199	652
306	Bleadon Hill	176	577
317	Glastonbury Tor	158	518
323	Brent Knoll	139	456

Notes
1. Also named Black Down
2. Also named Loxton Hill
3. Site of hill fort

32. Salisbury Plain

Top No	Name	Metres	Feet
158	Long Knoll	288	944
162	Brimsdown Hill	284	931
184	Wexcombe Down	267	875
215	White Sheet Hill	246	807
241	Westbury Hill	230	754
251	Sidbury Hill	223	731

Notes
1. Site of hill fort

Grid Reference	Ordnance Map 1/50k	1/25k	Notes
485573	182	1198	1.
540514	182/183	1198	
565488	182/183	1218	
442559	182	1198	
553667	172/182	1182	
665406	183	1219	
407559	182	1198	
666366	183	1239	
366571	182	1197	2.
513387	182/183	1238	3.
341509	182	1197	3.
786377	183	1239	
826392	183	1240	
278577	174	1202	
805347	183	1240	1.
901511	184	1200	
216506	184	1202	1.

Top No	Name	Height in Metres	Feet

33. North Downs

Top No	Name	Metres	Feet
175	Gibbet Hill	272	892
183	Botley Hill	267	875
205	Betsom's Hill	251	823
225	Sundridge Hill	240	787
231	Near Cooper's Wood	235	770
232	Reigate Hill	235	770
245	Hackhurst Downs	226	741
249	Holybourne Down	225	738
260	Brockham Hill	215+	705+
282	Near Thurnham	200+	656+
304	Tolsford Hill	181	593
309	St Martha's Hill	175	574

Notes   1. Kent county top

34. Lundy Island

Top No	Name	Metres	Feet
322	Acklands Moor	142	465

35. Quantock Hills

Top No	Name	Metres	Feet
83	Wills Neck	384	1259
100	Lydeard Hill	365	1197
103	Hurley Beacon	358	1174
134	Beacon Hill	310	1017
155	Broomfield Hill	290	951

Grid Reference	Ordnance Map 1/50k	1/25k	Notes
900359	186	1245	
396553	187	1207	
435563	187	1208	1.
467584	188	1208	
593600	188	1192	
256521	187	1207	
112490	187	1226	
725436	186	1224	
195513	187	1206	
805586	188	1210	
160384	189	1252	
028483	186	1226	
132448	180	1213	
166352	181	1236	
180343	181	1236	
148381	181	1216	
125410	181	1216	
215332	182	1237	

Top No	Name	Height in Metres	Feet

36. Brendon Hills

Top No	Name	Metres	Feet
49	Lype Hill	423	1387
56	Treborough Common	412	1351
78	Elworthy Barrows	394	1292
86	Withycombe Common	381	1249

Notes   1. Site of hill fort
            2. Also named Monkham Hill

37. Exmoor

Top No	Name	Metres	Feet
1	Five Barrows Hill	493	1617
3	The Chains	487	1597
32	Elsworthy	444	1456
46	Brightworthy Barrows	428	1404
47	Winsford Hill	426	1397
105	Haddon Hill	355	1164
107	Holdstone Down	349	1144
126	Great Hangman	318	1043
137	Selworthy Beacon	308	1010

Notes   1. Also named Western Common
            2. Summit site of barrow
            3. Also named Dry Hill
            4. Also named Withypool Common
            5. Summit is named Hadborough
            6. Also named Holdstone Hill

Grid Reference	Ordnance Map 1/50k	1/25k	Notes
950371	181	9	
005351	181	9	
070339	181	9	1.
987394	181	9	2.
732368	180	9	1.
735419	180	9	2.
812415	181	9	3.
819351	181	9	4.
877343	181	9	
961286	181	9	5.
619477	180	9	6.
601481	180	9	
919480	181	9	

Top No	Name	Height in Metres	Feet

38. Blackdown Hills

Top No	Name	Metres	Feet
129	Staple Hill	315	1033
166	Buckland Hill	280	918
177	Wellingham Hill	272	892
181	Black Down Common	268	879

39. Cranborne Chase

Top No	Name	Metres	Feet
172	Whin Green	277	908
186	Melbury Hill	263	862
187	Breeze Hill	262	859
223	White Sheet Hill	242	793
269	Duncliffe Hill	210	688
279	Fovent Down	201	659
301	Pentridge Hill	185	606

Notes   1. Summit is named Melbury Beacon
2. Chiselbury hill fort
3. Also named Pentbury Knoll

Grid Reference	Ordnance Map 1/50k	1/25k	Notes
240167	193	1278	
167177	181/193	1277	
137172	193	1277	
122163	181/193	1277	
925206	184	1261	
873197	183	1281	1.
899204	184	1261	
944242	184	1240	
826226	183	1261	
018281	184	1262	2.
041172	184	1282	3.

40. Dorset Chalk Hills

169	Lewesdon Hill	279	915
171	Pilsdon Pen	277	908
173	Wooland Hill	274	898
185	Gore Hill	265	869
189	Giant Hill	261	856
194	Bell Hill	258	846
199	Lambert's Castle Hill	256	838
228	Black Down	237	777
289	Corton Hill	194	636
293	Hambledon Hill	192	629

Notes   1. Dorset county top
         2. Site of Cerne Abbas Giant
         3. Site of Thomas Hardy Monument
         4. Site of neolithic camp

438012	193	1298	
413011	193	1298	1.
778056	194	1299	
637039	194	1299	
674036	194	1299	2.
800083	194	1300	
370988	193	1316	
613876	194	1332	3.
633234	183	1260	
848122	194	1281	4.

41. South Downs

165	Blackdown Hill	280	918
179	Butser Hill	270	885
201	Littleton Down	253	830
208	Ditchling Beacon	248	813
209	Linch Ball	248	813
211	Wheatham Hill	248	813
217	Burton Down	245	803
221	Beacon Hill	242	793
226	Chanctonbury Hill	238	780
234	Wether Down	234	767
236	Heyshott Down	233	764
247	Bignor Hill	225	738
255	Firle Beacon	217	711
256	Fulking Hill	217	711
259	Truleigh Hill	216	708
262	Wilmington Hill	214	702
263	Kithurst Hill	213	698
265	Old Winchester Hill	212	695
268	West Hill	211	692
270	Barlavington Down	208	682
271	Blackcap	206	675
272	St Roche's Hill	206	675
273	Wolstonbury Hill	206	675
278	Beacon Hill	201	659
280	Willington Hill	201	659
283	Castle Hill	200	656
291	Combe Hill	193	633
292	Rackham Hill	193	633
307	Cheesefoot Head	176	577
313	Beachy Head	164	538
314	Cliffe Hill	164	538

Notes   1. West Sussex county top
        2. East Sussex county top
        3. Also named Linch Down, site of hill fort

919296	197	1266	1.
717203	197	1265	
941149	197	1286	
331131	198	1288	2.
848174	197	1286	3.
741272	186/197	1265	
966131	197	1286	
807184	197	1286	4.
134120	198	1287	4.
675198	185	1285	
900166	197	1286	
981132	197	1286	
486059	198	1308	
258108	198	1288	5.
226108	198	1288	
548034	199	1324	6.
082125	197	1287	
648195	185	1265	4.
279117	198	1288	
962156	197	1286	
374125	198	1288	
878110	197	1286	
284138	198	1288	4.
603224	185	1265	
577009	199	1324	
374075	198	1307	
577022	199	1324	
053126	197	1287	
531277	185	1264	
591968	199	1324	
434107	198	1289	

4. Site of hill fort
5. Also named Devil's Dyke (Hill)
6. Also named Windover Hill, site of Long Man

Top No	Name	Height in Metres	Feet

42. Surrey

150	Leith Hill	295	967

Notes   1. Surrey county top

43. The Weald

248	Greenwood Gate Clump	225	738
276	Saxonbury Hill	203	666

44. Dartmoor

2	Penn Moor	493	1617
6	Belstone Tor	479	1571
11	Rippon Tor	473	1551
17	Ugborough Moor	464	1522
33	Bellever Tor	443	1453

Notes   1. Also named Shell Top
             2. Also named Belstone Common

45. Devon

252	Horner Hill	222	728

Grid Reference	Ordnance Map 1/50k	1/25k	Notes
139432	187	1226	1.
474310	188	1248	
578330	188	1248	
602646	202	28	1.
614920	191	28	2.
746756	191	28	
653626	202	28	
645764	191	28	
251021	193	1297	

Top No	Name	Height in	
		Metres	*Feet*

46. Purbeck Hills

Top No	Name	Metres	Feet
277	Swyre Head	203	666
285	Nine Barrow Down	199	652
287	Ridgeway Hill	198	652
288	Povington Hill	195+	639+
303	Whiteway Hill	185	606
311	Bindon Hill	168	551
316	Ballard Down	162	531

47. Isle of Wight

Top No	Name	Metres	Feet
224	St Boniface Down	240+	787+
229	St Catherine's Hill	237	777
233	Shanklin Down	235	770
246	Stenbury Down	226	740
261	Brightstone Down	214	702
320	Tennyson Down	147	482
326	Bembridge Down	104	341

Notes   1. Site of St Catherine's Oratory
2. Also named Appuldurcombe Down
3. Site of Tennyson's Monument
4. Site of Bembridge Fort

Grid Reference	Ordnance Map 1/50k	1/25k	Notes
934786	195	15	
008812	195	15	
915818	195	15	
888811	194	15	
877810	194	15	
840803	194	15	
025813	195	15	
569785	196	29	
494773	196	29	1.
568802	196	29	
536796	196	29	2.
432847	196	29	
325853	196	29	3.
625860	196	29	4.

Top No	Name	Height in Metres	Feet

48. Bodmin Moor

Top No	Name	Metres	Feet
51	Brown Willy	420	1377
70	Little Rough Tor	400	1312
74	Twelve Men's Tor	396	1299
85	Stow's Hill	381	1249
91	Caradon Hill	371	1217
110	Bray Down	346	1135
113	Brown Gelly	342	1122
117	Kit Hill	334	1095
119	Garrow Downs	330	1082
136	Condolden Barrow	308	1010
138	Hawk's Tor	307	1007

Notes   1. Cornwall county top
             2. Also named Kilmar Tor
             3. Also named Garrow Tor

49. St Austell Moors

Top No	Name	Metres	Feet
133	Hensbarrow Beacon	312	1023
242	Belowda Beacon	227	744
257	Castle Downs	216	708
258	St Breock Downs	216	708
294	St Agnes Beacon	192	629

50. West Penwith Moors

Top No	Name	Metres	Feet
204	Watch Croft	252	826
212	Tendrine Hill	247	810
250	Bartinney Downs	224	734
266	Trink Hill	212	695

Grid Reference	Ordnance Map 1/50k	1/25k	Notes
159800	201	1338	1.
145808	200	1325	
253749	201	1339	2.
258725	201	1339	
273707	201	1339	
189822	201	1325	
196727	201	1338	
375713	201	1339	
145785	200	1338	3.
090872	190/200	1325	
141756	200	1338	
997575	200	1353	
971626	200	1346	
946623	200	1346	
968682	200	1346	
710502	203	1352	
421357	203	1364	
479387	203	1364	
395293	203	1368	
505372	203	1364	

Top No	Name	Height in Metres	Feet

51. Carn Menellis Moor

202	Carnmenellis	252	826

52. Goonhilly Downs

324	Dry Tree	113	370

Notes   1. Site of satellite earth station

53. Isles of Scilly

331	Point 49 St Marys Island	49	160

54. Anglesea

254	Holyhead Mountain	220	721
319	Parys Mountain	147	482

55. Clwydian Hills

14	Moel Gyw	467	1532
16	Moel Llys-y-coed	465	1525
21	Moel Arthur	456	1496
36	Moel y Plâs	440	1443
37	Penycloddiau	440	1443
40	Moel Eithinen	434	1423
55	Moel y Waun	412	1351
75	Warren	396	1299

Notes   1. Site of hill fort

| Grid Reference | Ordnance Map | | Notes |
	1/50k	1/25k	
696365	203	1365	
725211	204	1369	1.
912121	203	25	
219829	114	734	
443905	114	733	
171575	116	788	
152654	116	772	
145661	116	772	1.
170554	116	788	
127679	116	772	1.
167592	116	788	
169534	116	788	
119700	116	772	

Top No	Name	Height in	
		Metres	*Feet*

56. Lleyn Peninsular

| 92 | Carn Fadryn | 371 | 1217 |

57. Breidden Hills

63	Moel y Golfa	403	1322
96	Middletown Hill	367	1204
98	Breidden Hill	365	1197

Notes   1. Site of hill fort
              2. Site of Rodney's Pillar

58. Preseli

13	Cerrig Lladron	468	1535
64	Carn Siân	402	1318
76	Frenni Fawr	395	1295
99	Carn Menyn	365	1197
101	Foeldrygarn	363	1190
108	Mynydd Carningli	347	1138
109	Mynydd Castlebythe	347	1138
116	Mynydd Cilciffeth	335	1099
139	Mynydd Dinas	307	1007

Notes   1. Also named Foel Eryr
              2. Site of ancient settlement
              3. Summit is named Carn Ingli
              4. Summit is named Garn Fawr

Grid Reference	Ordnance Map		Notes
	1/50k	*1/25k*	
279352	123	821	
291126	126	868	
306134	126	868	1.
295145	126	868	2.
066321	145	1033	1.
128321	145	1033	
203349	145	1034	
144325	145	1033	
158336	145	1033	2.
063372	145	1033	3.
029297	145/157	1057	
010324	145/157	1033	
007369	145/157	1033	4.

Top No	Name	Height in Metres	Feet

59. Radnor Forest

| 31 | Carneddau | 445 | 1459 |

60. Mynydd Eppynt

| 8 | Mynydd Eppynt | 478 | 1568 |

61. Black Mountains

| 4 | Ysgyryd Fawr | 486 | 1594 |

Notes   1. Also named The Skirrid

62. Gower Peninsular

297	Cefn Bryn	188	616
299	Llanmadoc Hill	186	610
302	Rhossili Down	185	606

Grid Reference	Ordnance Map		Notes
	1/50k	1/25k	
070552	147	992	
961464	147	1014	
331183	161	13	1.
518889	159	1126	
430924	159	1126	
418901	159	1126	

TABLE OF THE NOTABLE HILL TOPS OF ENGLAND AND WALES
IN ORDER OF ALTITUDE

Top No	Name	Group
1	Five Barrows Hill	Exmoor
2	Penn Moor	Dartmoor
3	The Chains	Exmoor
4	Ysgyryd Fawr	Black Mountains
5	Simon's Seat	Ingleborough
6	Belstone Tor	Dartmoor
7	Hoofe Stones Height	South Pennines
8	Mynydd Eppynt	Mynydd Eppynt
9	Lose Hill	Peak District
10	Top of Leach	South Pennines
11	Rippon Tor	Dartmoor
12	Blackstone Edge	South Pennines
13	Cerrig Lladron	Preseli
14	Moel Gyw	Clwydian Hills
15	Birkin Clough Head	South Pennines
16	Moel Llys-y-coed	Clwydian Hills
17	Ugborough Moor	Dartmoor
18	Winhill Pike	Peak District
19	Caer Caradoc Hill	Long Mynd
20	High Neb	Peak District
21	Moel Arthur	Clwydian Hills
22	Winter Hill	South Pennines
23	Ramshaw Rocks	Peak District
24	Round Hill	South Pennines
25	Round Hill	North York Moors
26	Trough Edge End	South Pennines
27	Dick Delf Hill	South Pennines
28	Nab Hill	South Pennines
29	Thieveley Pike	South Pennines
30	White Hill	South Pennines
31	Carneddau	Radnor Forest

Height in Metres	Date Ascended/Notes
493	_____
493	_____
487	_____
486	_____
485	_____
479	_____
479	_____
478	_____
476	_____
474	_____
473	_____
472	_____
468	_____
467	_____
465+	_____
465	_____
464	_____
462	_____
459	_____
458	_____
456	_____
456	_____
455+	_____
455+	_____
454	_____
454	_____
452	_____
451	_____
449	_____
446	_____
445	_____

Top No	Name	Group
32	Elsworthy	Exmoor
33	Bellever Tor	Dartmoor
34	Wolf Stones	South Pennines
35	Carr and Crags Moor	South Pennines
36	Moel y Plâs	Clwydian Hills
37	Penycloddiau	Clwydian Hills
38	Tosson Hill	Simonside Hills
39	Dog Hill	South Pennines
40	Moel Eithinen	Clwydian Hills
41	Stony Ridge	North York Moors
42	Cringle Moor	North York Moors
43	Danby High Moor	North York Moors
44	Simonside	Simonside Hills
45	Rosedale Head	North York Moors
46	Brightworthy Barrows	Exmoor
47	Winsford Hill	Exmoor
48	Worcester Beacon	Malverns
49	Lype Hill	Brendon Hills
50	High Wheeldon	Peak District
51	Brown Willy	Bodmin Moor
52	Bull Hill	South Pennines
53	Manshead End	South Pennines
54	Durham Edge	Peak District
55	Moel y Waun	Clwydian Hills
56	Treborough Common	Brendon Hills
57	Hen Cloud	Peak District
58	Great Hameldon	South Pennines
59	Long Mountain	Long Mynd
60	Gunner's Box	Simonside Hills
61	TheWrekin	Long Mynd
62	Noon Hill	North York Moors
63	Moel y Golfa	Breidden Hills
64	Carn Siân	Preseli
65	Rombald's Moor	South Pennines

Height in Metres	Date Ascended/Notes
444	_____
443	_____
443	_____
441	_____
440	_____
440	_____
440	_____
435	_____
434	_____
434	_____
432	_____
432	_____
430	_____
429	_____
428	_____
426	_____
425	_____
423	_____
422	_____
420	_____
418	_____
417	_____
416	_____
412	_____
412	_____
410	_____
409	_____
408	_____
407	_____
407	_____
404	_____
403	_____
402	_____
402	_____

Top No	Name	Group
66	Stoodley Pike	South Pennines
67	Sutton Common	Peak District
68	Black Hambleton	North York Moors
69	Brown Wardle Hill	South Pennines
70	Little Rough Tor	Bodmin Moor
71	Ragleth Hill	Long Mynd
72	White Hill	North York Moors
73	North Hill	Malverns
74	Twelve Men's Tor	Bodmin Moor
75	Warren	Clwydian Hills
76	Frenni Fawr	Preseli
77	Waddington Fell	Bowland Forest
78	Elworthy Barrows	Brendon Hills
79	Hope Bowdler Hill	Long Mynd
80	Wolfscote Hill	Peak District
81	Cold Moor	North York Moors
82	Gun	Peak District
83	Wills Neck	Quantock Hills
84	Blakey Ridge	North York Moors
85	Stow's Hill	Bodmin Moor
86	Withycombe Common	Brendon Hills
87	The Lawley	Long Mynd
88	Golden Heights	North York Moors
89	Little Moor	North York Moors
90	Beeley Moor	Peak District
91	Caradon Hill	Bodmin Moor
92	Carn Fadryn	Lleyn Peninsular
93	Weaver Hill	Peak District
94	Roundton Hill	Long Mynd
95	Ecton Hill	Peak District
96	Middletown Hill	Breidden Hills
97	White Edge	Peak District
98	Breidden Hill	Breidden Hills
99	Carn Menyn	Preseli

Height in Metres	Date Ascended/Notes
402	_____
402	_____
400	_____
400	_____
400	_____
398	_____
398	_____
397	_____
396	_____
396	_____
395	_____
395	_____
394	_____
393	_____
388	_____
385	_____
385	_____
384	_____
383	_____
381	_____
381	_____
377	_____
376	_____
374	_____
371	_____
371	_____
371	_____
371	_____
370	_____
369	_____
367	_____
366	_____
365	_____
365	_____

Top No	Name	Group
100	Lydeard Hill	Quantock Hills
101	Foeldrygarn	Preseli
102	Coal Hill	North York Moors
103	Hurley Beacon	Quantock Hills
104	Wetton Hill	Peak District
105	Haddon Hill	Exmoor
106	Soles Hill	Peak District
107	Holdstone Down	Exmoor
108	Mynydd Carningli	Preseli
109	Mynydd Castlebythe	Preseli
110	Bray Down	Bodmin Moor
111	Melkridge Common	Hadrian's Wall
112	The Cloud	Peak District
113	Brown Gelly	Bodmin Moor
114	Hereford Beacon	Malverns
115	Callow Hill	Long Mynd
116	Mynydd Cilciffeth	Preseli
117	Kit Hill	Bodmin Moor
118	Cleeve Hill	Cotswolds
119	Garrow Downs	Bodmin Moor
120	Helmsley Bank	North York Moors
121	Hob on the Hill	North York Moors
122	Beacon Batch	Mendips
123	Earl's Hill	Long Mynd
124	Roseberry Topping	North York Moors
125	Broadway Hill	Cotswolds
126	Great Hangman	Exmoor
127	Diddlebury Common	Long Mynd
128	Hepburn Moor	Cheviots
129	Staple Hill	Blackdown Hills
130	Walton Hill	Clent Hills
131	High Barn	North York Moors
132	Kerridge Hill	Peak District
133	Hensbarrow Beacon	St Austell Moors

Height in Metres	Date Ascended/Notes
365	_____
363	_____
360	_____
358	_____
358	_____
355	_____
355	_____
349	_____
347	_____
347	_____
346	_____
345	_____
343	_____
342	_____
338	_____
335+	_____
335	_____
334	_____
330	_____
330	_____
328	_____
328	_____
325	_____
320	_____
320	_____
319	_____
318	_____
317	_____
315	_____
315	_____
315	_____
313	_____
313	_____
312	_____

Top No	Name	Group
134	Beacon Hill	Quantock Hills
135	Adam's Hill	Clent Hills
136	Condolden Barrow	Bodmin Moor
137	Selworthy Beacon	Exmoor
138	Hawk's Tor	Bodmin Moor
139	Mynydd Dinas	Preseli
140	North Hill	Mendips
141	Pen Hill	Mendips
142	Brimham Rocks	North Yorkshire
143	Bredon Hill	Cotswolds
144	Stony Leas	North York Moors
145	Beacon Hill	Lickey Hills
146	Sutton Bank	North York Moors
147	Birdlip Hill	Cotswolds
148	Walbury Hill	Hampshire Downs
149	May Hill	Forest of Dean
150	Leith Hill	Surrey
151	Milk Hill	Marlborough Downs
152	Tan Hill	Marlborough Downs
153	Leckhampton Hill	Cotswolds
154	Inkpen Hill	Hampshire Downs
155	Broomfield Hill	Quantock Hills
156	Ruardean Hill	Forest of Dean
157	Martinsell Hill	Marlborough Downs
158	Long Knoll	Salisbury Plain
159	Waseley Hill	Lickey Hills
160	Midsummer Hill	Malverns
161	Pilot Hill	Hampshire Downs
162	Brimsdown Hill	Salisbury Plain
163	Painswick Beacon	Cotswolds
164	Wenlock Edge	Long Mynd
165	Blackdown Hill	South Downs
166	Buckland Hill	Blackdown Hills
167	Bardon Hill	Charnwood Forest

Height in Metres	Date Ascended/Notes
310	_____
309	_____
308	_____
308	_____
307	_____
307	_____
307	_____
305	_____
301	_____
299	_____
299	_____
298	_____
298	_____
297	_____
297	_____
296	_____
295	_____
294	_____
294	_____
293	_____
290+	_____
290	_____
290	_____
289	_____
288	_____
287	_____
286	_____
286	_____
284	_____
283	_____
280+	_____
280	_____
280	_____
279	_____

Top No	Name	Group
168	Buck Stone	Forest of Dean
169	Lewesdon Hill	Dorset Chalk Hills
170	Liddington Hill	Marlborough Downs
171	Pilsdon Pen	Dorset Chalk Hills
172	Whin Green	Cranborne Chase
173	Wooland Hill	Dorset Chalk Hills
174	Crickley Hill	Cotswolds
175	Gibbet Hill	North Downs
176	Hackpen Hill	Marlborough Downs
177	Wellingham Hill	Blackdown Hills
178	Golden Ball Hill	Marlborough Downs
179	Butser Hill	South Downs
180	Barbury Hill	Marlborough Downs
181	Black Down Common	Blackdown Hills
182	Aston Hill	Chilterns
183	Botley Hill	North Downs
184	Wexcombe Down	Salisbury Plain
185	Gore Hill	Dorset Chalk Hills
186	Melbury Hill	Cranborne Chase
187	Breeze Hill	Cranborne Chase
188	Beacon Hill	Hampshire Downs
189	Giant Hill	Dorset Chalk Hills
190	Ilmington Down	Cotswolds
191	Uffington Hill	Lambourn Downs
192	Coombe Hill	Chilterns
193	Morgan's Hill	Marlborough Downs
194	Bell Hill	Dorset Chalk Hills
195	Cherhill Down	Marlborough Downs
196	Haydown Hill	Hampshire Downs
197	Bald Hill	Chilterns
198	Haresfield Hill	Cotswolds
199	Lambert's Castle Hill	Dorset Chalk Hills
200	Charlbury Hill	Lambourn Downs
201	Littleton Down	South Downs

Height in Metres	Date Ascended/Notes
279	_____
279	_____
277	_____
277	_____
277	_____
274	_____
273	_____
272	_____
272	_____
272	_____
270+	_____
270	_____
268	_____
268	_____
267	_____
267	_____
267	_____
265	_____
263	_____
262	_____
261	_____
261	_____
261	_____
261	_____
260	_____
260	_____
258	_____
258	_____
258	_____
257	_____
256	_____
256	_____
253	_____
253	_____

Top No	Name	Group
202	Carnmenellis	Carn Menellis Moor
203	Little Down	Hampshire Downs
204	Watch Croft	West Penwith Moors
205	Betsom's Hill	North Downs
206	Kymin	Forest of Dean
207	Beacon Hill	Charnwood Forest
208	Ditchling Beacon	South Downs
209	Linch Ball	South Downs
210	Pulpit Hill	Chilterns
211	Wheatham Hill	South Downs
212	Tendrine Hill	West Penwith Moors
213	Coombe Down	Marlborough Downs
214	Cot Nab	Yorkshire Wolds
215	White Sheet Hill	Salisbury Plain
216	Callow Hill	Mendips
217	Burton Down	South Downs
218	Sparshalt Down	Lambourn Downs
219	Wain Hill	Chilterns
220	Dunstable Down	Chilterns
221	Beacon Hill	South Downs
222	Castle Hill	Cannock Chase
223	White Sheet Hill	Cranborne Chase
224	St Boniface Down	Isle of Wight
225	Sundridge Hill	North Downs
226	Chanctonbury Hill	South Downs
227	Birdsall Brow	Yorkshire Wolds
228	Black Down	Dorset Chalk Hills
229	St Catherine's Hill	Isle of Wight
230	Watership Down	Hampshire Downs
231	Near Cooper's Wood	North Downs
232	Reigate Hill	North Downs
233	Shanklin Down	Isle of Wight
234	Wether Down	South Downs
235	Dundry Hill	Mendips

Height in Metres	Date Ascended/Notes
252	_____
252	_____
252	_____
251	_____
250+	_____
248	_____
248	_____
248	_____
248	_____
248	_____
247	_____
246	_____
246	_____
246	_____
245+	_____
245	_____
244	_____
244	_____
243	_____
242	_____
242	_____
242	_____
240+	_____
240	_____
238	_____
237	_____
237	_____
237	_____
237	_____
235	_____
235	_____
235	_____
234	_____
233	_____

Top No	Name	Group
236	Heyshott Down	South Downs
237	Brailes Hill	Cotswolds
238	Ladle Hill	Hampshire Downs
239	Beacon Hill	Chilterns
240	Dover's Hill	Cotswolds
241	Westbury Hill	Salisbury Plain
242	Belowda Beacon	St Austell Moors
243	Crowberry Tump	Lambourn Downs
244	Raw Head	Peckforton Hills
245	Hackhurst Downs	North Downs
246	Stenbury Down	Isle of Wight
247	Bignor Hill	South Downs
248	Greenwood Gate Clump	The Weald
249	Holybourne Down	North Downs
250	Bartinney Downs	West Penwith Moors
251	Sidbury Hill	Salisbury Plain
252	Horner Hill	Devon
253	Small Down Knoll	Mendips
254	Holyhead Mountain	Anglesea
255	Firle Beacon	South Downs
256	Fulking Hill	South Downs
257	Castle Downs	St Austell Moors
258	St Breock Downs	St Austell Moors
259	Truleigh Hill	South Downs
260	Brockham Hill	North Downs
261	Brightstone Down	Isle of Wight
262	Wilmington Hill	South Downs
263	Kithurst Hill	South Downs
264	Maiden Castle	Peckforton Hills
265	Old Winchester Hill	South Downs
266	Trink Hill	West Penwith Moors
267	Wavering Down	Mendips
268	West Hill	South Downs
269	Duncliffe Hill	Cranborne Chase

Height in Metres	Date Ascended/Notes
233	_____
232	_____
232	_____
230	_____
230	_____
230	_____
227	_____
227	_____
227	_____
226	_____
226	_____
225	_____
225	_____
225	_____
224	_____
223	_____
222	_____
222	_____
220	_____
217	_____
217	_____
216	_____
216	_____
216	_____
215+	_____
214	_____
214	_____
213	_____
212	_____
212	_____
212	_____
211	_____
211	_____
210	_____

Top No	Name	Group
270	Barlavington Down	South Downs
271	Blackcap	South Downs
272	St Roche's Hill	South Downs
273	Wolstonbury Hill	South Downs
274	Cuckhamsley Hill	Berkshire Downs
275	Nibley Knoll	Cotswolds
276	Saxonbury Hill	The Weald
277	Swyre Head	Purbeck Hills
278	Beacon Hill	South Downs
279	Fovent Down	Cranborne Chase
280	Willington Hill	South Downs
281	Coppet Hill	Forest of Dean
282	Near Thurnham	North Downs
283	Castle Hill	South Downs
284	Creech Hill	Mendips
285	Nine Barrow Down	Purbeck Hills
286	Muswell Hill	Chilterns
287	Ridgeway Hill	Purbeck Hills
288	Povington Hill	Purbeck Hills
289	Corton Hill	Dorset Chalk Hills
290	Meon Hill	Cotswolds
291	Combe Hill	South Downs
292	Rackham Hill	South Downs
293	Hambledon Hill	Dorset Chalk Hills
294	St Agnes Beacon	St Austell Moors
295	Chase End Hill	Malverns
296	Heslerton Wold	Yorkshire Wolds
297	Cefn Bryn	Gower Peninsular
298	Quainton Hill	Chilterns
299	Llanmadoc Hill	Gower Peninsular
300	Lowbury Hill	Berkshire Downs
301	Pentridge Hill	Cranborne Chase
302	Rhossili Down	Gower Peninsular
303	Whiteway Hill	Purbeck Hills

Height in Metres	Date Ascended/Notes
208	_____
206	_____
206	_____
206	_____
203	_____
203	_____
203	_____
203	_____
201	_____
201	_____
201	_____
200+	_____
200+	_____
200	_____
199	_____
199	_____
198	_____
198	_____
195	_____
194	_____
194	_____
193	_____
193	_____
192	_____
192	_____
191	_____
190	_____
188	_____
187	_____
186	_____
186	_____
185	_____
185	_____
185	_____

Top No	Name	Group
304	Tolsford Hill	North Downs
305	Staxton Wold	Yorkshire Wolds
306	Bleadon Hill	Mendips
307	Cheesefoot Head	South Downs
308	Potter Brompton Wold	Yorkshire Wolds
309	St Martha's Hill	North Downs
310	Yearsley Moor	Howardian Hills
311	Bindon Hill	Purbeck Hills
312	Normaby-le-wold	Lincolnshire Wolds
313	Beachy Head	South Downs
314	Cliffe Hill	South Downs
315	Halidon Hill	Berwick upon Tweed
316	Ballard Down	Purbeck Hills
317	Glastonbury Tor	Mendips
318	High Street	Lincolnshire Wolds
319	Parys Mountain	Anglesea
320	Tennyson Down	Isle of Wight
321	Danebury Hill	Hampshire Downs
322	Acklands Moor	Lundy Island
323	Brent Knoll	Mendips
324	Dry Tree	Goonhilly Downs
325	Leadenham Heath	Lincolnshire Edge
326	Bembridge Down	Isle of Wight
327	Saxby Wolds	Lincolnshire Wolds
328	Somerby Top	Lincolnshire Wolds
329	Barn Hill	London
330	Horsendon Hill	London
331	Point 49 St Marys Island	Isles of Scilly
332	Ongar Hill	Norfolk

Height in Metres	Date Ascended/Notes
181	_____
178	_____
176	_____
176	_____
176	_____
175	_____
174	_____
168	_____
168	_____
164	_____
164	_____
163	_____
162	_____
158	_____
149	_____
147	_____
147	_____
143	_____
142	_____
139	_____
113	_____
105+	_____
104	_____
102	_____
97	_____
86	_____
85	_____
49	_____
4	_____

TABLE OF THE NOTABLE HILL TOPS IN ALPHABETICAL ORDER

Name	Top No
Acklands Moor	322
Adam's Hill	135
Aston Hill	182
Bald Hill	197
Ballard Down	316
Barbury Hill	180
Bardon Hill	167
Barlavington Down	270
Barn Hill	329
Bartinney Downs	250
Beachy Head	313
Beacon Batch	122
Beacon Hill (Charnwood Forest)	207
Beacon Hill (Chilterns)	239
Beacon Hill (Hampshire Downs)	188
Beacon Hill (Lickey Hills)	145
Beacon Hill (Quantock Hills)	134
Beacon Hill (South Downs)	221
Beacon Hill (South Downs)	278
Beeley Moor	90
Bell Hill	194
Bellever Tor	33
Belowda Beacon	242
Belstone Tor	6
Bembridge Down	326
Betsom's Hill	205
Bignor Hill	247
Bindon Hill	311
Birdlip Hill	147
Birdsall Brow	227
Birkin Clough Head	15
Black Down	228

Name	Top No
Black Down Common	181
Black Hambleton	68
Blackcap	271
Blackdown Hill	165
Blackstone Edge	12
Blakey Ridge	84
Bleadon Hill	306
Botley Hill	183
Brailes Hill	237
Bray Down	110
Bredon Hill	143
Breeze Hill	187
Breidden Hill	98
Brent Knoll	323
Brightstone Down	261
Brightworthy Barrows	46
Brimham Rocks	142
Brimsdown Hill	162
Broadway Hill	125
Brockham Hill	260
Broomfield Hill	155
Brown Gelly	113
Brown Wardle Hill	69
Brown Willy	51
Buck Stone	168
Buckland Hill	166
Bull Hill	52
Burton Down	217
Butser Hill	179
Caer Caradoc Hill	19
Callow Hill (Long Mynd)	115
Callow Hill (Mendips)	216

Name	*Top No*
Cuckhamsley Hill	274
Danby High Moor	43
Danebury Hill	321
Dick Delf Hill	27
Diddlebury Common	127
Ditchling Beacon	208
Dog Hill	39
Dover's Hill	240
Dry Tree	324
Duncliffe Hill	269
Dundry Hill	235
Dunstable Down	220
Durham Edge	54
Earl's Hill	123
Ecton Hill	95
Elsworthy	32
Elworthy Barrows	78
Firle Beacon	255
Five Barrows Hill	1
Foeldrygarn	101
Fovent Down	279
Frenni Fawr	76
Fulking Hill	256
Garrow Downs	119
Giant Hill	189
Gibbet Hill	175
Glastonbury Tor	317
Golden Ball Hill	178
Golden Heights	88
Gore Hill	185
Great Hameldon	58
Great Hangman	126
Greenwood Gate Clump	248
Gun	82

Name	Top No
Kymin	206
Ladle Hill	238
Lambert's Castle Hill	199
Lawley The	87
Leadenham Heath	325
Leckhampton Hill	153
Leith Hill	150
Lewesdon Hill	169
Liddington Hill	170
Linch Ball	209
Little Down	203
Little Moor	89
Little Rough Tor	70
Littleton Down	201
Llanmadoc Hill	299
Long Knoll	158
Long Mountain	59
Lose Hill	9
Lowbury Hill	300
Lydeard Hill	100
Lype Hill	49
Maiden Castle	264
Manshead End	53
Martinsell Hill	157
May Hill	149
Melbury Hill	186
Melkridge Common	111
Meon Hill	290
Middletown Hill	96
Midsummer Hill	160
Milk Hill	151
Moel Arthur	21
Moel Eithinen	40
Moel Gyw	14

Name	Top No
Moel Llys-y-coed	16
Moel y Golfa	63
Moel y Plâs	36
Moel y Waun	55
Morgan's Hill	193
Muswell Hill	286
Mynydd Carningli	108
Mynydd Castlebythe	109
Mynydd Cilciffeth	116
Mynydd Dinas	139
Mynydd Eppynt	8
Nab Hill	28
Near Cooper's Wood	231
Near Thurnham	282
Nibley Knoll	275
Nine Barrow Down	285
Noon Hill	62
Normaby-le-wold	312
North Hill (Malverns)	73
North Hill (Mendips)	140
Old Winchester Hill	265
Ongar Hill	332
Painswick Beacon	163
Parys Mountain	319
Pen Hill	141
Penn Moor	2
Pentridge Hill	301
Penycloddiau	37
Pilot Hill	161
Pilsdon Pen	171
Point 49 St Marys	331
Potter Brompton Wold	308
Povington Hill	288
Pulpit Hill	210

Name	*Top No*
Quainton Hill	298
Rackham Hill	292
Ragleth Hill	71
Ramshaw Rocks	23
Raw Head	244
Reigate Hill	232
Rhossili Down	302
Ridgeway Hill	287
Rippon Tor	11
Rombald's Moor	65
Roseberry Topping	124
Rosedale Head	45
Round Hill (North Yorks Moors)	25
Round Hill (South Pennines)	24
Roundton	94
Ruardean Hill	156
Saxby Wolds	327
Saxonbury Hill	276
Selworthy Beacon	137
Shanklin Down	233
Sidbury Hill	251
Simonside	44
Simon's Seat	5
Small Down Knoll	253
Soles Hill	106
Somerby Top	328
Sparshalt Down	218
St Agnes Beacon	294
St Boniface Down	224
St Breock Downs	258
St Catherine's Hill	229
St Martha's Hill	309
St Roche's Hill	272
Staple Hill	129

Name	Top No
Wellingham Hill	177
Wenlock Edge	164
West Hill	268
Westbury Hill	241
Wether Down	234
Wetton Hill	104
Wexcombe Down	184
Wheatham Hill	211
Whin Green	172
White Edge	97
White Hill (North York Moors)	72
White Hill (South Pennines)	30
White Sheet Hill (Cranborne Chase)	223
White Sheet Hill (Salisbury Plain)	215
Whiteway Hill	303
Willington Hill	280
Wills Neck	83
Wilmington Hill	262
Winhill Pike	18
Winsford Hill	47
Winter Hill	22
Withycombe Common	86
Wolf Stones	34
Wolfscote Hill	80
Wolstonbury Hill	273
Wooland Hill	173
Worcester Beacon	48
Wrekin The	61
Yearsley Moor	310
Ysgyryd Fawr	4

ANALYSIS OF THE NOTABLE HILL TOPS BY GROUPS AND AREAS

Area	*Group*	*No of Tops*
England:	1. Berwick upon Tweed	1
	2. Cheviots	1
	3. Simonside Hills	3
	4. Hadrian's Wall	1
	5. North York Moors	19
	6. Yorkshire Wolds	5
	7. Howardian Hills	1
	8. Ingleborough	1
	9. North Yorkshire	1
	10. Forest of Bowland	1
	11. South Pennines	20
	12. Lincolnshire Wolds	4
	13. Lincolnshire Edge	1
	14. Peak District	18
	15. Peckforton Hills	2
	16. Norfolk	1
	17. Cannock Chase	1
	18. Charnwood Forest	2
	19. Long Mynd	11
	20. Clent Hills	2
	21. Lickey Hills	2
	22. Malvern Hills	5
	23. Cotswolds	13
	24. Forest of Dean	5
	25. Chilterns	9
	26. Lambourn Downs	4
	27. Marlborough Downs	10
	28. Berkshire Downs	2
	29. London	2
	30. Hampshire Downs	9
	31. Mendips	11
	32. Salisbury Plain	6

Area	*Group*	*No of Tops*
	33. North Downs	12
	34. Lundy Island	1
	35. Quantock Hills	5
	36. Brendon Hills	4
	37. Exmoor	9
	38. Blackdown Hills	4
	39 Cranbourne Chase	7
	40. Dorset Chalk Hills	10
	41. South Downs	31
	42. Surry	1
	43. The Weald	2
	44. Dartmoor	5
	45. Devon	1
	46. Purbeck Hills	7
	47. Isle of Wight	7
	48. Bodmin Moor	11
	49. St Austell Moors	5
	50. West Penwith Moors	4
	51. Carn Menellis Moor	1
	52. Goonhilly Downs	1
	53. Isles of Scilly	1
	Total	**303**

Wales:	54. Anglesea	2
	55. Clwydian Hills	8
	56. Lleyn Peninsular	1
	57. Breidden Hills	3
	58. Preseli	9
	59. Radnor Forest	1
	60. Mynydd Eppynt	1
	61. Black Mountains	1
	62. Gower Peninsular	3
	Total	**29**

Breakdown by height bands

450 - 499m	28
400 - 449m	42
350 - 399m	36
300 - 349m	36
250 - 299m	64
200 - 249m	77
150 - 199m	34
100 - 149m	10
below 100m	5
Total	**332**

Chapter 4

The County Tops of England and Wales

INTRODUCTION

I must admit that I have not visited all the county tops; it is not a common challenge, but I thought it might be of interest. Some county tops are not tops at all, but points on a rising hillside: the county top of Avon, for example, is situated on the northern slopes of the Mendip Hills. Two counties, Greater Manchester and Wiltshire, have the honour of having two county tops both of identical height.

A number of county tops are on or near metalled roads and I believe you should start from a valley floor or low point and walk up to the top. For example Ilmington Down, the county top of Warwickshire, is on an unclassified road and the route I took started from the village of Mickledon, lying at the foot of the Cotswold escarpment.

One inherent problem with the county tops list is, "how long will it remain current"? Some of the new counties designated by the 1974 Boundary Commission will certainly disappear in the next few years. The much unloved county of Cleveland, for instance, may go, with its component parts returning to Yorkshire and Lincolnshire.

TABLE OF THE COUNTY TOPS OF ENGLAND AND WALES

No	County	Name
1	Avon	Near Nett Wood Farm
2	Bedfordshire	Dunstable Down
3	Berkshire	Walbury Hill
4	Buckinghamshire	Aston Hill
5	Cambridgeshire	Near Great Chishill
6	Cheshire	Shining Tor
7	Cleveland	Hob on the Hill
8	Cornwall	Brown Willy
9	Cumbria	Scafell Pike
10	Derbyshire	Kinder Scout
11	Devon	High Willhays
12	Dorsetshire	Pilsdon Pen
13	Durham	Mickle Fell
14	East Sussex	Ditchling Beacon
15	Essex	Pickerton Green
16	Gloucestershire	Cleeve Hill
17	Greater London	Betsom's Hill
18a	Greater Manchester	Featherbed Moss
18b	Greater Manchester	Black Chew Head

Notes

1. Near East Harptree on Mendip Hills
2. Chiltern Hills
3. Berkshire Downs
4. Chiltern Hills
5. Summit is east of village on B1039 road
6. Peak District
7. Cleveland Hills
8. Bodmin Moor
9. Cumbrian Mountains

Height in		Grid	Ordnance Map	
Metres	Feet	Ref	1/50k	1/25k
264	866	565539	182/183	1198
243	797	009194	166	1095
297	974	374616	174	1186
267	875	890090	165	1118
146	479	426385	154	1050
559	1833	995737	118	24
328	1076	634123	94	26
420	1378	159800	201	1338
978	3208	216072	89/90	6
636	2086	086875	110	1
621	2037	580892	191	28
277	908	413011	193	22
788	2585	804243	91/92	31
248	813	331131	198	1288
147	482	443362	154	1050
330	1082	997246	163	1066
246	807	435565	187	1208
541	1775	046012	110	1
541	1775	056028	110	1

10. Peak District
11. Dartmoor
12. Dorset Chalk Hills
13. Northern Pennines
14. South Downs
16. Cotswolds
17. North Downs
18a. Peak District
18b. Second top of same height in county

No	County	Name
19	Hampshire	Pilot Hill
20	Hereford & Worcester	Black Mountain
21	Hertfordshire	Near Hastoe
22	Humberside	Cot Nab
23	Isle of Wight	St Boniface Down
24	Kent	Betsom's Hill
25	Lancashire	Green Hill
26	Leicestershire	Bardon Hill
27	Lincolnshire	Normanby-le-wold
28	Merseyside	Billinge Hill
29	Norfolk	Beacon Hill
30	Northamptonshire	Arlbury Hill
31	Northumberland	The Cheviot
32	North Yorkshire	Whernside
33	Nottinghamshire	Herrod's Hill
34	Oxfordshire	Bald Hill
35	Shropshire	Brown Clee Hill
36	Somerset	Dunkery Beacon

Notes

19. Berkshire Downs
20. Black Mountains, summit on Welsh border
21. Chilterns
22. The Yorkshire Wolds
24. North Downs
25. Yorkshire Dales
26. Charnwood Forest
27. The Lincolnshire Wolds

| Height in | | Grid | Ordnance Map | |
Metres	Feet	Ref	1/50k	1/25k
286	938	398601	174	1186
703	2306	255355	161	13
244	800	914092	165	1118
246	807	821570	106	666
240+	787+	560785	196	29
251	823	436563	187	1208
628	2060	702820	98	2
278	912	460132	129	874
168	551	121964	113	730
179	587	526014	108	711
102	334	185413	133	820
225	738	540587	152	999
815	2673	909205	74/75	475
736	2414	738814	98	2
201	659	462597	120	795
257	843	729958	165	1137
540	1771	594867	137/138	931
519	1702	891416	181	9

31. Cheviots
32. Yorkshire Dales
34. Chilterns
35. The Long Mynd, summit is named Abdon Burf
36. Exmoor

	nty	Name
	uth Yorkshire	Howdon Edge
	affordshire	Oliver Hill
	uffolk	Elm's Farm
40	Surrey	Leith Hill
41	Tyne and Wear	Leadgate near Chopwell
42	Warwickshire	Ilmington Down
43	West Midlands	Turner's Hill
44	West Sussex	Blackdown Hill
45	West Yorkshire	Black Hill
46a	Wiltshire	Milk Hill
46b	Wiltshire	Tan Hill
47	Clwyd	Cadair Berwyn - South Top
48	Dyfyd	West of Fan Foel
49	Gwent	Chwarel y Fan
50	Gwynydd	Yr Wyddfa (Snowdon)
51	Mid Glamorgan	Near Cefnffordd
52	Powys	Pen y Fan
53	South Glamorgan	Craig Llysfaen
54	West Glamorgan	Cefnffordd

Notes

37. Peak District, summit is named High Stones
38. Peak District
42. Cotswolds
44. North Downs
45. Peak District
46a. Marlborough Downs
46b. Second top of same height in county
47. Berwyns

Height in		Grid	Ordnance Map	
Metres	Feet	Ref	1/50k	1/25k
550	1804	188944	110	1
513	1683	027676	119	24
128	419	787559	155	1005
295	967	139432	187	1226
259	849	107593	88	561
261	856	188426	151	1020
271	889	968887	139	933
280	918	919296	197	1266
582	1909	078047	110	1
294	964	104641	173	1185
294	964	082647	173	1185
830	2723	072323	125	826
770+	2526+	821223	160	12
679	2227	258294	161	13
1085	3559	610544	115	17
590+	1935+	905031	170	1108
886	2906	012216	160	11
264	866	190851	171	1148
600	1968	907032	170	1108

48. Brecon Beacons, Camarthen Fan
49. Black Mountains
50. Snowdon
51. Brecon Beacons
52. Brecon Beacons
53. Top 2.5 miles WSW of Caerphilly
54. Brecon Beacons, also named Craig-y-llyn

TABLE OF THE COUNTY TOPS IN ORDER OF ALTITUDE

County	Name
Gwynydd	Yr Wyddfa (Snowdon)
Cumbria	Scafell Pike
Powys	Pen y Fan
Clwyd	Cadair Berwyn - South Top
Northumberland	The Cheviot
Durham	Mickle Fell
Dyfyd	West of Fan Foel
North Yorkshire	Whernside
Hereford & Worcester	Black Mountain
Gwent	Chwarel y Fan
Derbyshire	Kinder Scout
Lancashire	Green Hill
Devon	High Willhays
West Glamorgan	Cefnffordd
Mid Glamorgan	Near Cefnffordd
West Yorkshire	Black Hill
Cheshire	Shining Tor
South Yorkshire	Howdon Edge
Greater Manchester	Black Chew Head
Greater Manchester	Featherbed Moss
Shropshire	Brown Clee Hill
Somerset	Dunkery Beacon
Staffordshire	Oliver Hill
Cornwall	Brown Willy
Gloucestershire	Cleeve Hill
Cleveland	Hob on the Hill
Berkshire	Walbury Hill
Surrey	Leith Hill
Wiltshire	Milk Hill
Wiltshire	Tan Hill
Hampshire	Pilot Hill
West Sussex	Blackdown Hill

Height	Date Visited
1085	_____
978	_____
886	_____
830	_____
815	_____
788	_____
770+	_____
736	_____
703	_____
679	_____
636	_____
628	_____
621	_____
600	_____
590+	_____
582	_____
559	_____
550	_____
541	_____
541	_____
540	_____
519	_____
513	_____
420	_____
330	_____
328	_____
297	_____
295	_____
294	_____
294	_____
286	_____
280	_____

County	*Name*
Leicestershire	Bardon Hill
Dorsetshire	Pilsdon Pen
West Midlands	Turner's Hill
Buckinghamshire	Near Aston Hill
Avon	Near Nett Wood Farm
South Glamorgan	Craig Llysfaen
Warwickshire	Ilmington Down
Tyne and Wear	Leadgate near Chopwell
Oxfordshire	Bald Hill
Kent	Betsom's Hill
East Sussex	Ditchling Beacon
Greater London	Betsom's Hill
Humberside	Cot Nab
Hertfordshire	Near Hastoe
Bedfordshire	Dunstable Down
Isle of Wight	St Boniface Down
Northamptonshire	Arlbury Hill
Nottinghamshire	Herrod's Hill
Merseyside	Billinge Hill
Lincolnshire	Normanby-le-wold
Essex	Pickerton Green
Cambridgeshire	Near Great Chishill
Suffolk	Elm's Farm
Norfolk	Beacon Hill

Height	*Date Visited*
278	_____
277	_____
271	_____
267	_____
264	_____
264	_____
261	_____
259	_____
257	_____
251	_____
248	_____
246	_____
246	_____
244	_____
243	_____
240+	_____
225	_____
201	_____
179	_____
168	_____
147	_____
146	_____
128	_____
102	_____

Cleeve Hill, Cotswolds – Gloucestershire county top (*Author*)

Chapter 5

Wainwright's Lake District Fells

INTRODUCTION

The Wainwrght series of guide books with their detailed drawings and handwritten descriptions have become a favourite with hill-walkers over the years. Many people use his guide books for planning their routes on the Lakeland fells. During my visits to the Lake District I have met many hill-walkers who were "doing the Wainwrights", on one occasion I met a local walker who was on his second round. For all you Wainwright's fans, this chapter is dedicated to his Lake District fells.

WAINWRIGHT'S PICTORIAL GUIDES TO THE LAKELAND FELLS:

Book 1 - The Eastern Fells
Book 2 - The Far Eastern Fells
Book 3 - The Central Fells
Book 4 - The Southern Fells
Book 5 - The Northern Fells
Book 6 - The North Western Fells
Book 7 - The Western Fells

TABLE OF WAINWRIGHT'S LAKE DISTRICT FELLS IN BOOK ORDER

Book 1 - The Eastern Fells

Top No	Name	Height in Metres	Feet
W1	Arnison Crag	433	1420
W2	Birkhouse Moor	718	2355
W3	Birks	622	2040
W4	Catstycam	890	2919
W5	Clough Head	726	2381
W6	Dollywaggon Pike	858	2814
W7	Dove Crag	792	2598
W8	Fairfield	873	2864
W9	Glenridding Dodd	442	1450
W10	Gowbarrow Fell	481	1578
W11	Great Dodd	857	2811
W12	Great Mell Fell	537	1761
W13	Great Rigg	766	2513
W14	Hart Crag	822	2696
W15	Hart Side	756	2480
W16	Hartsop above How	580+	1902+
W17	Helvellyn	950	3116
W18	Heron Pike	612	2007
W19	High Hartsop Dodd	519	1702
W20	High Pike	656	2152

Notes

1. Also named Catstye Cam or Catchedicam
2. Also named White Pike
3. Summit is named Greatrigg Man
4. Also named Scandale Fell

Grid Reference	Ordnance Map 1/50k	1/25k	Notes
394150	90	5	
364159	90	5	
380143	90	5	
348158	90	5	1.
334226	90	5	2.
346131	90	5	
375105	90	5/7	
359118	90	5	
381176	90	5	
408218	90	5	
342206	90	5	
397254	90	5	
356104	90	5/7	3.
368113	90	5	
359197	90	5	
383120	90	5	
342152	90	5	
356083	90	7	
394108	90	5/7	
374088	90	7	4.

Book 1 - The Eastern Fells (continued)

Top No	Name	Height in Metres	Feet
W21	Little Hart Crag	637	2089
W22	Little Mell Fell	505	1656
W23	Low Pike	508	1666
W24	Middle Dodd	654	2145
W25	Nab Scar	440+	1443+
W26	Nethermost Pike	891	2923
W27	Raise	883	2896
W28	Red Screes	776	2545
W29	Saint Sunday Crag	841	2759
W30	Seat Sandal	736	2414
W31	Sheffield Pike	675	2214
W32	Stone Arthur	500+	1640+
W33	Stybarrow Dodd	843	2765
W34	Watson's Dodd	789	2588
W35	White Side	863	2831

Notes

5. Also named Kilnshaw Chimney
6. Summit is named The Cape
7. Also named Arthur's Chair
8. Summit is named Whiteside Bank

Grid Reference	Ordnance Map 1/50k	1/25k	Notes
387101	90	5/7	
423240	90	5	
374078	90	7	
397096	90	5/7	
356071	90	7	
344142	90	5	
343174	90	5	
397088	90	7	5.
369134	90	5	6.
344115	90	5	
369182	90	5/7	
348092	90	7	7.
343189	90	5	
336196	90	5	
338167	90	5	8.

Book 2 - The Far Eastern Fells

Top No	Name	Height in Metres	Feet
W36	Angletarn Pikes	567	1860
W37	Arthur's Pike	530+	1738+
W38	Beda Fell	509	1669
W39	Bonscale Pike	520+	1706+
W40	Branstree	713	2339
W41	Brock Crags	561	1840
W42	Caudale Moor	763	2503
W43	Froswick	720	2362
W44	Gray Crag	699	2293
W45	Grey Crag	638	2093
W46	Hallin Fell	388	1272
W47	Harter Fell	778	2552
W48	Hartsop Dodd	618	2027
W49	High Raise	802	2631
W50	High Street	828	2716
W51	Ill Bell	757	2483
W52	Kentmere Pike	730	2394
W53	Kidsty Pike	780+	2559+
W54	The Knott	739	2454
W55	Loadpot Hill	671	2201
W56	Mardale Ill Bell	760	2493
W57	The Nab	576	1889
W58	Place Fell	657	2155

Notes

1. Summit is named Beda Head
2. Also named Swarth Fell or Toughmoss Pike
3. Also named Brant Street or Artlecrag Pike
4. Also named Stony Cove Pike or John Bell's Banner
5. Also named Hill Bell

Grid Reference	Ordnance Map 1/50k	1/25k	Notes
413148	90	5	
461207	90	5	
428171	90	5	1.
454201	90	5	2.
478100	90	5/7	3.
419137	90	5	
418100	90	5/7	4.
435085	90	7	
428117	90	5	
497072	90	7	
433198	90	5	
460093	90	5/7	
411118	90	5	
448135	90	5	
441111	90	5	
437077	90	7	5.
466078	90	7	
448126	90	5	
437127	90	5	
457181	90	5	
448101	90	5/7	
434152	90	5	
406170	90	5	

Book 2 - The Far Eastern Fells (continued)

Top No	Name	Height in Metres	Feet
W59	Rampsgill Head	792	2598
W60	Rest Dodd	696	2283
W61	Sallows	516	1692
W62	Selside Pike	655	2148
W63	Shipman Knotts	587	1925
W64	Sour Howes	483	1584
W65	Steel Knotts	432	1417
W66	Tarn Crag	664	2178
W67	Thornthwaite Crag	784	2572
W68	Troutbeck Tongue	364	1194
W69	Wansfell	484	1587
W70	Wether Hill	670+	2198+
W71	Yoke	706	2316

Notes

6. Named Ramsgill Head on early OS maps
7. Also named Kentmere Park
8. Also named Applewaite Common
9. Summit named Pikeawassa
10. Also named Thornthwaite Beacon
11. Also named The Tongue or Troutbeck Park
12. Summit is named Wansfell Pike
13. Also named Weather Hill
14. Named Yolk on some OS maps

Grid Reference	Ordnance Map 1/50k	1/25k	Notes
443128	90	5	6.
433137	90	5	
437040	90	7	7.
490112	90	5	
473063	90	7	
428032	90	7	8.
440181	90	5	9.
488078	90	7	
432101	90	5/7	10.
423064	90	7	11.
394042	90	7	12.
455163	90	5	13.
438067	90	7	14.

Book 3 - The Central Fells

Top No	Name	Height in Metres	Feet
W72	Armboth Fell	479	1571
W73	Bleaberry Fell	590	1935
W74	Blea Rigg	540+	1771+
W75	Calf Crag	537	1761
W76	Eagle Crag	520+	1706+
W77	Gibson Knott	420+	1377+
W78	Grange Fell	410+	1345+
W79	Great Crag	440+	1443+
W80	Harrison Stickle	736	2414
W81	Helm Crag	405	1328
W82	High Raise	762	2500
W83	High Rigg	343	1125
W84	High Seat	608	1994
W85	High Tove	515	1689
W86	Loft Crag	680+	2230+
W87	Loughrigg Fell	335	1099
W88	Pavey Ark	700+	2296+
W89	Pike o' Stickle	709	2326
W90	Raven Crag	461	1512
W91	Sergeant Man	730+	2394+
W92	Sergeant's Crag	571	1873
W93	Silver How	390+	1279+
W94	Steel Fell	553	1814
W95	Tarn Crag	540+	1771+
W96	Thunacar Knott	723	2372
W97	Ullscarf	726	2381
W98	Walla Crag	379	1243

Notes

1. Also named Brund Fell or Jopplety How
2. Affectionately known as The Lion and The Lamb
3. Summit is named High White Stones

Grid Reference	Ordnance Map 1/50k	1/25k	Notes
297159	89/90	4	
286196	89/90	4	
302078	90	6/7	
302104	90	4/6	
276121	89/90	4	
319099	90	4/6/7	
264162	89/90	4	1.
270147	89/90	4	
282074	89/90	6	
327093	90	4/5/6/7	2.
281095	89/90	4	3.
308215	90	4/5	
287181	89/90	4	
289165	89/90	4	
278071	89/90	6	
347051	90	7	
285079	89/90	6	
274074	89/90	6	4.
303187	90	4/5	
286089	89/90	6	
274114	89/90	4	
325066	90	6/7	
319112	90	4/5	5.
304092	90	4/6	
279080	89/90	6	
291122	89/90	4	
277213	90	4	6.

4. Named Pike of Stickle on OS maps
5. Summit is named Dead Pike
6. Named Wallow Crag on old OS maps

Book 4 - The Southern Fells

Top No	Name	Height in Metres	Feet
W99	Allan Crags	785	2575
W100	Black Fell	323	1059
W101	Bowfell	902	2959
W102	Brim Fell	796	2611
W103	Cold Pike	701	2299
W104	Coniston Old Man	803	2634
W105	Crinkle Crags	859	2818
W106	Dow Crag	778	2552
W107	Esk Pike	885	2903
W108	Glaramara	783	2568
W109	Great Carrs	785	2575
W110	Great End	910	2985
W111	Green Crag	489	1604
W112	Grey Friar	770+	2526+
W113	Hard Knott	549	1801
W114	Harter Fell	653	2142

Notes

1. Named Bow Fell on present OS maps
2. Properly The Old Man of Coniston
3. Summit is named Long Top
4. Also named Ulpha Fell

Grid Reference	Ordnance Map 1/50k	1/25k	Notes
237085	89/90	6	
340016	90	7	
245064	89/90	6	1.
271986	96/97	6	
263036	89/90	6	
272978	96/97	6	2.
249049	89/90	6	3.
263978	96/97	6	
237075	89/90	6	
246105	89/90	4/6	
271009	89/90	6	
227084	89/90	6	
200983	96	6	4.
260004	89/90	6	
232024	90	6	
219997	96	6	

Book 4 - The Southern Fells (continued)

Top No	Name	Height in Metres	Feet
W115	Holme Fell	317	1040
W116	Illgill Head	609	1998
W117	Lingmell	800+	2624+
W118	Lingmoor Fell	469	1538
W119	Pike o' Blisco	705	2312
W120	Rossett Pike	651	2135
W121	Rosthwaite Fell	548	1797
W122	Scafell	964	3162
W123	Scafell Pike	978	3208
W124	Seathwaite Fell	632	2073
W125	Slight Side	762	2500
W126	Swirl How	802	2631
W127	Wetherlam	762	2500
W128	Whin Rigg	535	1755

Notes

5. Also referred to as Wastwater Screes
6. Summit is named Brown Howe
7. Named Pike of Blisco on OS maps
8. Summit is named Bessyboot
9. Formerly Scawfell or Scaw Fell
10. Cumbria county top, formally The Pikes of Scawfell
11. Summit is named Little Walls

Grid Reference	Ordnance Map 1/50k	1/25k	Notes
315006	90	6/7	
169049	89	6	5.
209082	89/90	6	
303046	90	6/7	6.
271042	89/90	6	7.
249076	89/90	6	
258125	89/90	4	8.
207065	89/90	6	9.
216072	89/90	6	10.
227097	89/90	4/6	
210050	89/90	6	
273005	89/90	6	
288011	89/90	6	11.
152034	89	6	

Book 5 - The Northern Fells

Top No	Name	Height in Metres	Feet
W129	Bakestall	673	2207
W130	Bannerdale Crags	683	2240
W131	Binsey	447	1466
W132	Blencathra	868	2847
W133	Bowscale Fell	702	2303
W134	Brae Fell	586	1922
W135	Carl Side	746	2447
W136	Carrock Fell	660+	2165+
W137	Dodd	502	1646
W138	Great Calva	690	2263
W139	Great Cockup	526	1725
W140	Great Sca Fell	651	2135
W141	High Pike	658	2158
W142	Knott	710	2329
W143	Latrigg	368	1207
W144	Longlands Fell	483	1584
W145	Long Side	734	2408
W146	Lonscale Fell	715	2345
W147	Meal Fell	550	1804
W148	Mungrisdale Common	633	2076
W149	Skiddaw	931	3054
W150	Skiddaw Little Man	865	2837
W151	Souther Fell	522	1712
W152	Ullock Pike	690	2263

Notes

1. Also named Saddleback, summit is named Hallsfell Top
2. Also named Skiddaw Dodd, Little Dodd or Dodd Fell
3. Summit is named Longside Edge
4. Summit is named Skiddaw Man
5. Also named Low Man or Little Man

Grid Reference	Ordnance Map 1/50k	1/25k	Notes
266307	89/90	576	
335290	90	5	
225355	89/90	576	
323277	90	4/5	1.
333306	90	576	
289352	89/90	576	
255281	89/90	4	
342336	90	576	
244274	89/90	4	2.
291312	89/90	576	
273333	89/90	576	
291339	89/90	576	
319350	90	576	
296330	89/90	576	
279247	89/90	4	
276354	89/90	576	
248284	89/90	4	3.
285272	89/90	4	
283337	89/90	576	
312292	90	4/5	
261291	89/90	4	4.
267278	89/90	4	5.
355292	90	5	
244288	89/90	4	

Book 6 - The North Western Fells

Top No	Name	Height in Metres	Feet
W153	Ard Crags	581	1906
W154	Barf	468	1535
W155	Barrow	455	1492
W156	Broom Fell	511	1676
W157	Castle Crag	290	951
W158	Catbells	451	1479
W159	Causey Pike	637	2089
W160	Dale Head	753	2470
W161	Eel Crag	839	2752
W162	Grasmoor	852	2795
W163	Graystones	456	1496
W164	Grisedale Pike	791	2595
W165	High Spy	653	2142
W166	Hindscarth	727	2385
W167	Hopegill Head	770	2526
W168	Knott Rigg	556	1824
W169	Ling Fell	373	1223
W170	Lord's Seat	552	1811
W171	Maiden Moor	576	1889
W172	Outerside	568	1863
W173	Rannerdale Knotts	355	1164
W174	Robinson	737	2417
W175	Sail	773	2536
W176	Sale Fell	359	1177
W177	Scar Crags	672	2204
W178	Wandope	772	2532
W179	Whinlatter	525	1722
W180	Whiteless Pike	660	2165
W181	Whiteside	707	2319

Notes

1. Also named Crag Fell
2. Also named Scawdel Fell, Eel Crags or Lobstone Band
3. Also named Hobcarton Pike

Grid Reference	Ordnance Map 1/50k	1/25k	Notes
207198	89/90	4	
214268	89/90	4	
227218	89/90	4	
195270	89/90	4	
249159	89/90	4	
244199	89/90	4	
219209	89/90	4	
223153	89/90	4	
193204	89/90	4	1.
175203	89/90	4	
178264	89/90	4	
198225	89/90	4	
234162	89/90	4	2.
216165	89/90	4	
186221	89/90	4	3.
197189	89/90	4	
180286	89/90	4	
204266	89/90	4	
237182	89/90	4	
211215	89/90	4	
167183	89	4	
202169	89/90	4	
198203	89/90	4	
194297	89/90	4	
208207	89/90	4	
188197	89/90	4	4.
197249	89/90	4	5.
180189	89/90	4	
171219	89/90	4	

4. Also known as Wanlope
5. Summit named Whinlatter Top

Book 7 - The Western Fells

Top No	Name	Height in Metres	Feet
W182	Base Brown	646	2119
W183	Blake Fell	573	1879
W184	Brandreth	715	2345
W185	Buckbarrow	420+	1377+
W186	Burnbank Fell	475	1558
W187	Caw Fell	690+	2263+
W188	Crag Fell	523	1715
W189	Fellbarrow	416	1364
W190	Fleetwith Pike	648	2125
W191	Gavel Fell	526	1725
W192	Great Borne	616	2020
W193	Great Gable	899	2949
W194	Green Gable	801	2627
W195	Grey Knotts	697	2286
W196	Grike	488	1601
W197	Haycock	797	2614
W198	Haystacks	597	1958
W199	Hen Comb	509	1669
W200	High Crag	744	2440

Notes

1. Also named Herdus or Herdhouse
2. Properly named Hay Stacks

Grid Reference	Ordnance Map 1/50k	1/25k	Notes
225115	89/90	4	
111197	89	4	
215119	89/90	4	
136061	89	6	
110209	89	4	
132109	89	4/6	
097144	89	4	
132242	89	4	
206142	89/90	4	
117185	89	4	
124164	89	4	1.
211103	89/90	4/6	
215107	89/90	4/6	
217126	89/90	4	
085141	89	4	
145107	89	4/6	
193132	89/90	4	2.
132181	89	4	
180140	89/90	4	

Book 7 - The Western Fells (continued)

Top No	Name	Height in Metres	Feet
W201	High Stile	807	2647
W202	Kirk Fell	802	2631
W203	Lank Rigg	541	1774
W204	Low Fell	423	1387
W205	Mellbreak	512	1679
W206	Middle Fell	582	1909
W207	Pillar	892	2926
W208	Red Pike (Buttermere)	755	2477
W209	Red Pike (Wasdale)	826	2709
W210	Scoat Fell	841	2759
W211	Seatallan	692	2270
W212	Starling Dodd	633	2076
W213	Steeple	819	2686
W214	Yewbarrow	628	2060

Notes

3. Also named Loweswater Fell
4. Also named Pillar Fell
5. Also named Little Scoat Fell
6. Formerly named Seat Allan

Grid Reference	Ordnance Map 1/50k	1/25k	Notes
170148	89/90	4	
195105	89/90	4/6	
092120	89	4	
137226	89	4	3.
149186	89	4	
151072	89	6	
171121	89/90	4	4.
161155	89	4	
165105	89	4/6	
160114	89	4	5.
139084	89	6	6.
142157	89	4	
157116	89	4	
173085	89/90	6	

TABLE OF WAINWRIGHT'S LAKE DISTRICT FELLS IN ORDER OF ALTITUDE

Top No	Book No	Name
W123	4	Scafell Pike
W122	4	Scafell
W17	1	Helvellyn
W149	5	Skiddaw
W110	4	Great End
W101	4	Bowfell
W193	7	Great Gable
W207	7	Pillar
W26	1	Nethermost Pike
W4	1	Catstycam
W107	4	Esk Pike
W27	1	Raise
W8	1	Fairfield
W132	5	Blencathra
W150	5	Skiddaw Little Man
W35	1	White Side
W105	4	Crinkle Crags
W6	1	Dollywaggon Pike
W11	1	Great Dodd
W162	6	Grasmoor
W33	1	Stybarrow Dodd
W29	1	Saint Sunday Crag
W210	7	Scoat Fell
W161	6	Eel Crag
W50	2	High Street
W209	7	Red Pike (Wasdale)
W14	1	Hart Crag
W213	7	Steeple
W201	7	High Stile
W104	4	Coniston Old Man
W49	2	High Raise

Height in Metres	Date Ascended/Notes
978	_____
964	_____
950	_____
931	_____
910	_____
902	_____
899	_____
892	_____
891	_____
890	_____
885	_____
883	_____
873	_____
868	_____
865	_____
863	_____
859	_____
858	_____
857	_____
852	_____
843	_____
841	_____
841	_____
839	_____
828	_____
826	_____
822	_____
819	_____
807	_____
803	_____
802	_____

Top No	Book No	Name
W202	7	Kirk Fell
W126	4	Swirl How
W194	7	Green Gable
W117	4	Lingmell
W197	7	Haycock
W102	4	Brim Fell
W7	1	Dove Crag
W59	2	Rampsgill Head
W164	6	Grisedale Pike
W34	1	Watson's Dodd
W99	4	Allan Crags
W109	4	Great Carrs
W67	2	Thornthwaite Crag
W108	4	Glaramara
W53	2	Kidsty Pike
W106	4	Dow Crag
W47	2	Harter Fell
W28	1	Red Screes
W175	6	Sail
W178	6	Wandope
W112	4	Grey Friar
W167	6	Hopegill Head
W13	1	Great Rigg
W42	2	Caudale Moor
W82	3	High Raise
W125	4	Slight Side
W127	4	Wetherlam
W56	2	Mardale Ill Bell
W51	2	Ill Bell
W15	1	Hart Side
W208	7	Red Pike (Buttermere)
W160	6	Dale Head
W135	5	Carl Side

Height in Metres	Date Ascended/Notes
802	_____
802	_____
801	_____
800+	_____
797	_____
796	_____
792	_____
792	_____
791	_____
789	_____
785	_____
785	_____
784	_____
783	_____
780+	_____
778	_____
778	_____
776	_____
773	_____
772	_____
770+	_____
770	_____
766	_____
763	_____
762	_____
762	_____
762	_____
760	_____
757	_____
756	_____
755	_____
753	_____
746	_____

Top No	Book No	Name
W200	7	High Crag
W54	2	The Knott
W174	6	Robinson
W80	3	Harrison Stickle
W30	1	Seat Sandal
W145	5	Long Side
W91	3	Sergeant Man
W52	2	Kentmere Pike
W166	6	Hindscarth
W5	1	Clough Head
W97	3	Ullscarf
W96	3	Thunacar Knott
W43	2	Froswick
W2	1	Birkhouse Moor
W184	7	Brandreth
W146	5	Lonscale Fell
W40	2	Branstree
W142	5	Knott
W89	3	Pike o' Stickle
W181	6	Whiteside
W71	2	Yoke
W119	3	Pike o' Blisco
W133	5	Bowscale Fell
W103	4	Cold Pike
W88	3	Pavey Ark
W44	2	Gray Crag
W195	7	Grey Knotts
W60	2	Rest Dodd
W211	7	Seatallan
W187	7	Caw Fell
W138	5	Great Calva
W152	5	Ullock Pike
W130	5	Bannerdale Crags

Height in Metres	Date Ascended/Notes
744	_____
739	_____
737	_____
736	_____
736	_____
734	_____
730+	_____
730	_____
727	_____
726	_____
726	_____
723	_____
720	_____
718	_____
715	_____
715	_____
713	_____
710	_____
709	_____
707	_____
706	_____
705	_____
702	_____
701	_____
700+	_____
699	_____
697	_____
696	_____
692	_____
690+	_____
690	_____
690	_____
683	_____

Top No	Book No	Name
W86	3	Loft Crag
W3	1	Sheffield Pike
W129	5	Bakestall
W177	6	Scar Crags
W55	2	Loadpot Hill
W70	2	Wether Hill
W66	2	Tarn Crag
W136	5	Carrock Fell
W180	6	Whiteless Pike
W141	5	High Pike
W58	2	Place Fell
W20	1	High Pike
W62	2	Selside Pike
W24	1	Middle Dodd
W114	4	Harter Fell
W165	6	High Spy
W140	5	Great Sca Fell
W120	4	Rossett Pike
W190	7	Fleetwith Pike
W182	7	Base Brown
W45	2	Grey Crag
W159	6	Causey Pike
W21	1	Little Hart Crag
W148	5	Mungrisdale Common
W212	7	Starling Dodd
W124	4	Seathwaite Fell
W214	7	Yewbarrow
W3	1	Birks
W48	2	Hartsop Dodd
W192	7	Great Borne
W18	1	Heron Pike
W116	4	Illgill Head
W84	3	High Seat

Height in Metres	Date Ascended/Notes
680+	_____
675	_____
673	_____
672	_____
671	_____
670+	_____
664	_____
660+	_____
660	_____
658	_____
657	_____
656	_____
655	_____
654	_____
653	_____
653	_____
651	_____
651	_____
648	_____
646	_____
638	_____
637	_____
637	_____
633	_____
633	_____
632	_____
628	_____
622	_____
618	_____
616	_____
612	_____
609	_____
608	_____

Top No	Book No	Name
W198	7	Haystacks
W73	3	Bleaberry Fell
W63	2	Shipman Knotts
W134	5	Brae Fell
W206	7	Middle Fell
W153	6	Ard Crags
W16	1	Hartsop above How
W171	6	Maiden Moor
W57	2	The Nab
W183	7	Blake Fell
W92	3	Sergeant's Crag
W172	6	Outerside
W36	2	Angletarn Pikes
W41	2	Brock Crags
W168	6	Knott Rigg
W94	3	Steel Fell
W170	6	Lord's Seat
W147	5	Meal Fell
W113	4	Hard Knott
W121	4	Rosthwaite Fell
W203	7	Lank Rigg
W74	3	Blea Rigg
W95	3	Tarn Crag
W75	3	Calf Crag
W12	1	Great Mell Fell
W128	4	Whin Rigg
W37	2	Arthur's Pike
W191	7	Gavel Fell
W139	5	Great Cockup
W179	6	Whinlatter
W188	7	Crag Fell
W151	5	Souther Fell
W39	2	Bonscale Pike

Height in Metres	Date Ascended/Notes
597	
590	
587	
586	
582	
581	
580+	
576	
576	
573	
571	
568	
567	
561	
556	
553	
552	
550	
549	
548	
541	
540+	
540+	
537	
537	
535	
530+	
526	
526	
525	
523	
522	
520+	

Top No	Book No	Name
W76	3	Eagle Crag
W19	1	High Hartsop Dodd
W61	2	Sallows
W85	3	High Tove
W205	7	Mellbreak
W156	6	Broom Fell
W38	2	Beda Fell
W199	7	Hen Comb
W23	1	Low Pike
W22	1	Little Mell Fell
W137	5	Dodd
W32	1	Stone Arthur
W111	4	Green Crag
W196	7	Grike
W69	2	Wansfell
W144	5	Longlands Fell
W64	2	Sour Howes
W10	1	Gowbarrow Fell
W72	3	Armboth Fell
W186	7	Burnbank Fell
W118	4	Lingmoor Fell
W154	6	Barf
W90	3	Raven Crag
W163	6	Graystones
W155	6	Barrow
W158	6	Catbells
W131	5	Binsey
W9	1	Glenridding Dodd
W79	3	Great Crag
W25	1	Nab Scar
W1	1	Arnison Crag
W65	2	Steel Knotts
W204	7	Low Fell

Height in Metres	Date Ascended/Notes
520+	_____
519	_____
516	_____
515	_____
512	_____
511	_____
509	_____
509	_____
508	_____
505	_____
502	_____
500+	_____
489	_____
488	_____
484	_____
483	_____
483	_____
481	_____
479	_____
475	_____
469	_____
468	_____
461	_____
456	_____
455	_____
451	_____
447	_____
442	_____
440+	_____
440+	_____
433	_____
432	_____
423	_____

Top No	Book No	Name
W185	7	Buckbarrow
W77	3	Gibson Knott
W189	7	Fellbarrow
W78	3	Grange Fell
W81	3	Helm Crag
W93	3	Silver How
W46	2	Hallin Fell
W98	3	Walla Crag
W169	6	Ling Fell
W143	5	Latrigg
W68	2	Troutbeck Tongue
W176	6	Sale Fell
W173	6	Rannerdale Knotts
W83	3	High Rigg
W87	3	Loughrigg Fell
W100	4	Black Fell
W115	4	Holme Fell
W157	6	Castle Crag

Height in Metres	Date Ascended/Notes
420+	_____
420+	_____
416	_____
410+	_____
405	_____
390+	_____
388	_____
379	_____
373	_____
368	_____
364	_____
359	_____
355	_____
343	_____
335	_____
323	_____
317	_____
290	_____

Glossary of Welsh Place Names

A little knowledge of Welsh place-names will help the reader to translate the some names of the Welsh mountains and hills.

Aber, river mouth
Adwy, pass, gap
Ael, brow or edge
Afon, river
Allt, wooded slope, cliff, or side of a hill
Aran, a high place
Arddu, black crag

Bach, Fach, little, small
Banc, bank, mound, hill
Banog, Bannog, elevated, conspicuous, horned
Bechan, Fechan, small - the lesser
Bedw, birch
Benllyn, head of a lake
Ber, a hilltop
Berfa, barrow
Bera, Bere, peak, top, point
Blaen, head of a valley
Boncen, Boncyn, Poncen, Poncyn, hillock, tump, bank
Boeth, Poeth, warm, hot
Bont, bridge
Braich, ridge, spur
Bran, Brain, crow, rook, raven
Brith, speckled
Bron, Fron, slope of a hill
Bronwen, white-breasted
Brycheiniog, Breconshire
Bryn, mound or hill

Bugeilyn, shepherds
Bwlch, pass or gap
Bychan, Fechan, small, little

Cadair, Gadair, chair or throne
Caer, camp or fortress
Calsh, lime, chalk
Canol, the middle one
Capel, chapel
Carn, a prominence or cairn
Carnedd, cairn, tumulus
Carreg, Cerreg, stone
Castell, a castle or fortress
Cefn, ridge
Cerwyn, tub, vat, winepress
Ceunant, ravine, gorge
Chwarel, quarry
Claer, clear, bright, shining
Clip, precipice, crag
Cloddiau, Cloddio, dig, quarry, mine
Clogwyn, cliff or precipice
Cnicht, knight
Coch, Goch, red
Coed, wood
Corn, peak, horn shape summit
Cors, bog or marshy place
Craig, Creigiau, Graig, crag
Crib, Grib, Cribin, Gribin, comb, ridge, crest
Cribin, the small crest of a hill

Croes, Groes, cross
Crug, heap or mound
Cwm, valley, hollow or coombe
Cyfrwy, ridge, saddle
Cyrniau, cones, cairns

Dafad, sheep, wart
Darren, knoll, rocky tump, rock-face
Ddelw, image
Dduallt, black spur or cliff
Ddysgl, dish
Dibyn, steep, precipice
Diffwys, precipice
Dinas, town or hill fort
Disgwylfa, watch tower
Dol, dale or meadow
Draws, Draw, yonder, away
Drosgl, rough hill
Drum, Trum, ridge
Drws, gap, door
Du, Ddu, Duon, black
Dŵr, water
Dwy, two
Dyffryn, wide valley
Dyfnant, ravine

Eglwys, Eglwysig, Eglwyseg, church, ecclesiastical
Eigiau, a shoal of fish
Eilio, to plait or weave
Elen, fawn
Eryi Eryri, highland, especially Snowdonia
Esgair, shank or limb

Fach, Bach, little, small

Faen, stone
Faes, field
Fan, peak, crest
Fawn, Mawn, peat bog, peaty
Fawr, Mawr, great, large
Fechan, Bychan, small, little
Felen, Melyn, yellow
Ffridd, plantation or mountain enclosure
Ffin, boundary
Ffordd, way, road
Fforchog, forked, forked streams
Ffynnon, fountain or well
Fign, Mign, bog
Filiast, greyhound bitch
Foel Moel, bare or bald hill
Fron, Bron, rounded hill
Fynydd, Mynydd, mountain

Gadair, Cadair, seat, chair
Gaer, camp or fortress
Gallt, slope, hillside
Garn, prominence, cairn
Garnedd, Carnedd, cairn, tumulus
Garreg, gareg, stone, rock
Garth, enclosure
Garw, course, rough
Geifr, goat
Glan, bank, shore
Glân, Clean, holy, fair
Glas, blue, green, grey, silver
Gleision, whey
Glyn, glen, valley
Goch, Coch, red
Godor, hindrance, delay
Godre, skirt, border, edge
Gorllwyn, ambush

Gors, swamp
Gorsedd, throne
Grach, scabby
Grib, Crib, Gribin, Cribin, comb, ridge, crest
Groes, Croes, cross
Gron, gravel
Grug, heather
Gwastad, plain
Gwaun, Waun, common, moor
Gwern, swamp, bog
Gwr, man, husband
Gwryd, fathom
Gwyliwr, watchman
Gwyn, white
Gwyntog, wind

Hafod, summer dwelling
Hen, old, aged
Hebog, hawk
Helgi, Helgi-du, hunting dog, black hunting dog
Helyg, willows
Hen, old
Hir, long
Hirnant, long valley
Hydd, stag

Isaf, lowest

Las, Glas, green, blue
Lefn, Llefn, smooth
Llan, church, village
Llech, slate, stone slab
Llechog, slaty
Llechwedd, hillside
Lledr, wide, broad

Llefn, Lefn, smooth
Llethr, slope, slabs
Llithrig, slippery
Lliwedd, stained, coloured
Lloer, moon
Llugwy, bright stream
Llwybr, path
Llwyd, Lwyd, grey, brown
Llwyn, Llwyni, bush, grove
Llyfn, smooth
Llygad, eye, source of a stream
Llyn, lake
Llysiau, herbs

Maen, Faen, stone
Maes, Faes, open field, plain
Main, thin narrow
Manod, fine or driven snow
Marian, moraine, strand, holm
Mawn, Fawn, peat bog, peaty
Mawr, Fawr, big, great
Meirch, horse, stallion
Melyn, Felan, yellow
Mign, Fign, bog
Mignedd, bogs, quagmires
Miliast, Filiast, greyhound bitch
Mochyn, Moch, pig, pigs
Moel, Foel, bare or bald hill
Morfa, moor, fen, marsh
Morwynion, maid, virgin
Mwdwl, cock
Mynydd, Fynydd, mountain, moorland

Nant, brook, valley
Nedd, lice, nits
Niwl, mist, hill-fog

Nod, aim, mark
Nyth, nest

Oer, cold, exposed
Ogof, cave
Oleu-wen, white light, moonlight

Pant, hollow, valley
Pawl, pole, stake
Pen, head, top, summit
Pennant, head of a glen
Perfedd, Berfedd, middle, entrails
Picws, oatcake
Pig, point, spike, beak
Pistyll, waterfall
Poeth, Boeth, warm, hot
Poncen, Poncyn, Boncen, Boncyn,
   small hill
Pont, bridge
Porth, Borth, gateway, harbour
Pwll, pit, pool

Rhaedr, waterfall (anglisised as
   Rhayader)
Rhedyn, bracken
Rhestr, list, row
Rhiw, hill, slope, ascent
Rhos, moor, promontory
Rhudd, red, crimson
Rhwng, between, among
Rhyd, ford

Sarn, causeway, pavement
Siambre, chamber
Siglen, morass

Sir, county
Sych, dry

Tal, front, end
Tan, under, as far as
Tarren, knoll, rocky tump
Tarw, bull
Teg, Tegid, fair, beautiful
Tir, land, ground, territory
Tor, belly or break
Traws, across, yonder
Trum, Drum, ridge
Twmpa, tump, knoll
Twr Tyrau, tower, towers
Twyn, hillock, knoll
Ty, Dy, house
Uchaf, highest, upper
Ugain, twenty
Uwch, higher, above

Waun, Gwaun, moor
Wen, Gwyn, white
Wenallt, white hillside
Wrach, Gwrach, hag, witch
Wyddfa, cairn, tumulus
Wyn, white

Y, yr, the
Yn, Ym, in, at, into
Ymenyn, butter
Ysfa, sheepwalk
Ysgafell, ledge, brow
Ysgyfarnogod, hares, possessing
   hares
Ystrad, valley, river meadow
Ystwyth, winding, bending

Bibliography

1. MOUNTAIN LISTS

Bridge George: *The Mountains of England and Wales*
Gaston's Alpine Books, West Col Productions 1973

Buxton Chris   *The Mountain Summits of England and Wales*
and Lewis Gwyn:
Buxton & Lewis 1986 ISBN 0 9511723 0 1

Donaldson J C: *Munro's Tables*
The Scottish Mountaineering Trust, revision for 1984

Elmslie W T: *The Two Thousand Footers of England*
Journal of the Fell and Rock Climbing Club of the English Lake District
1933, pages 433 to 351

The Guinness Book of Answers 8th Edition (County Tops)
Guinness Publishing Ltd 1990 ISBN 0 85112 957 9

Nuttall John and Anne: *The Mountains of England and Wales*
Volume 1 - *England*, Cicerone Press 1989, ISBN 1 85284 036 6
Volume 2 - *Wales*, Cicerone Press 1990, ISBN 1 85284 037 4

Rooke-Corbett J: *Twenty Fives*
The Rucksack Club Journal, 1911 pages 61 to 65

Wall C W: *Mountaineering in Ireland*
Federation of Mountaineering Clubs of Ireland 1976

Wright Nick: *English Mountain Summits*
Robert Hale & Co Ltd 1974 ISBN 0 7091 4560 8

2. HILL WALKING BOOKS

Allen Bob: *On High Lakeland Fells*
Pic Publications 1987

Birkett Bill: *Classic Walks in Great Britain*
Oxford Illustrated Press 1989 ISBN 1 85509 203 4

Clear John: *Fifty Best Walks of Britain*
Guild Publishing 1988

Dillon Paddy: *The Mountains of Ireland*
Cicerone Press 1992   ISBN 1 85284 110 9

Dugdale Graham: *Remote Walks around Lakeland*
Westmoreland Gazette 1989 ISBN 0 902272 78 0

Griffin A. H: *Adventuring in Lakeland*
Robert Hale & Co Ltd 1980 ISBN 0 7091 8586 2

Marsh Terry: *The Mountains of Wales*
Hodder and Stoughton 1981 ISBN 0-340-34827-5

Millmore Paul: *South Downs Way*
Aurun Press 1990 ISBN 1 85410 099 8

Monkhouse Patrick: *On Foot in North Wales and The Peak*
Re-published by Diadem Books 1988 ISBN 0 906371 32 5

Poucher W A: *The Lakeland Peaks*, first published 1960
                              The Peak and Pennines, first published 1966
                              The Welsh Peaks, first published 1962
Constable & Co Ltd

Pyatt Edward C: *Mountains of Britain*
B. T. Batsford Ltd 1966

Sale Richard: *Best Walks in North Wales*
                                Best Walks in Southern Wales
Constable & Co Ltd 1990

Stevenson Tom: *Forbidden Land*
Manchester University Press 1989 ISBN 0 7190 2891

Styles Showell: *The Mountains of North Wales*
Victor Gollancz Ltd 1973 ISBN 0 575 01494 6

Unsworth Walt: *The High Fells of Lakeland*
Robert Hale & Co Ltd 1972

Wainwright A: *A Pictorial Guide to the Lakeland Fells*

        Book 1 -   *The Eastern Fells*, first published 1955
        Book 2 -   *The Far Eastern Fells*, first published 1957
        Book 3 -   *The Central Fells*, first published 1958
        Book 4 -   *The Southern Fells*, first published 1960
        Book 5 -   *The Northern Fells*, first published 1962
        Book 6 -   *The North Western Fells*, first published 1964
        Book 7 -   *The Western Fells*, first published 1966
        Walks on The Howgill Fells
        Pennine Way Companion, first published 1968
        Fellwalking with Wainwright, 1984
Michael Joseph Ltd, previously published by The Westmoreland Gazette

Wainwright A: *Memoirs of a Fellwanderer*
Michael Joseph Ltd 1993